Sparkle-Tudes!

Inspirations for
Creating Sparkling Attitudes

Quotes By and For Women

Kimberlee

Keep up your
Sparkle-tude!

much Love,

Sheryl L. Roush

Creative Communications
San Diego, California

A spark is a little thing,
yet it may rekindle the world.

Mary Farquar Tupper

ISBN # 1-880878-08-9

Published by Creative Communications
The publications division of Sparkle Presentations
Post Office Box 2373
La Mesa, California 91943 U.S.A.
Sheryl@SparklePresentations.com
www.SparklePresentations.com

Biblical quotes, cultural proverbs and sayings are used
randomly from various translations.

First Printing 2003
July 2004 Printing

Library of Congress Cataloging-in-Publication Data
Roush, Sheryl Lynn.
        Sparkle-Tudes: Inspirations for Creating Sparkling Attitudes
        Quotes By & For Women/Sheryl L. Roush
Includes index.
        ISBN # 1-880878-08-9

1. Self-Help
2. Inspirational
3. Womens Issues

Library of Congress Control Number: 2004091387

Cover Photograph by Wardene Weisser, Nature Photographer

Book Design by Sheryl Roush
Editing by Emily DeShazo
Cover Design and Production by Drew Design

Sparkle-Tudes!

Inspirations for
Creating Sparkling Attitudes

Quotes By and For Women

Compiled by

Sheryl L. Roush

Dedication

To those who have mentored the women of the world
to honor, respect and take care of Mother Earth.

If you want to get closer to God,
get closer to nature.

Wardene Weisser
internationally recognized nature photographer
capturing God's handiwork through her keen gifts,
as seen published in Arizona Highways, National Geographic,
Sunset, Zoo Nooz, and numerous others.

Her commitment to saving the California Condor was one such
successful effort to preserve nature for future generations to come.

Wardene died of Breast Cancer and requested donations be made
to equipment for early-detection of this deadly disease,
thus preserving the lives of others.

Author Sheryl Roush shown here only one month
before the passing, of her Aunt Wardene.

Each woman has a uniqueness,
reflected in the brilliance of her words and deeds.

This book is dedicated to its readers,
that you may browse these pages
and be inspired to be a
cheerleader of Sparkling Attitude.

May we all walk the planet with new hope,
greater acceptance and respect,
deeper appreciation for others and nature,
daily gratitude and reflections of love
in all we do.

Here's to your "Sparkle-Tude!™"

Let your light shine.

Shine within you
so that it can shine
on someone else.

Let your light shine.

Oprah Winfrey
O, The Oprah Magazine
March 2004

Table of Contents

Table of Contents

Table of Contents

Table of Contents

Table of Contents

Achievement

Having lost the election, I'm in good company.
—Iris Adam, Natural Law Party Candidate for Governor of California, 2002, 2003

Act as if it were impossible to fail.
—Dorothea Brande

Focus on the majesty and excitement of what might be.
Dare to dream the impossible dreams.
—Jo Condrill, Speaker, Author "Take Charge of Your Life:
Dare to Pursue Your Dreams, www.goalminds.com

If you really want something, work hard, take advantage of opportunities,
and never give up, you will find a way.
—Jane Goodall, Scientist and Researcher

We don't know who we are until we see what we can do.
— Martha Grimes

Never under-estimate the power of doing absolutely nothing.
—Cath Kachur, Speaker, Artist

I truly believe that life is a self-fulfilling prophecy.
If you can dream it, you can do it.
You need to prepare yourself and be persevering.
If you think you can, you can.
If you think you can't, you're right.
So setting goals is number one for me.
—Darlene Kerr, Executive Vice President and COO, Niagara Mohawk
Excerpt from interview "Playing with the Big Boys" by Debra Pestrak
www.MostPowerfulWomen.com

Achievement

The real winners in life are the people who look at every situation
with an expectation that they can make it work or make it better.
—Barbara Pletcher, Author

The whole point of getting things done
is knowing what to leave undone.
—Lady Stella Reading

Question:
If heaven exists and God greeted you, what would you like to be told?
Answer:
You done good, kid!
—Sharon Stone, as interviewed on Screen Actors Guild

Look at a day when you are supremely satisfied at the end.
It's not a day when you lounge around doing nothing;
it's when you've had everything to do, and you've done it.
—Margaret Thatcher

I was the kind nobody thought could make it.
I had a funny Boston accent. I couldn't pronounce my R's.
I wasn't a beauty.
—Barbara Walters

I can do all things through Christ that strengthens me.
—Martha R. Wilson

My philosophy is that not only are you responsible for your life,
but doing the best at this moment puts you in the best place
for the next moment.
—Oprah Winfrey

Aging

I'm not interested in age. People who tell me their age are silly.
You're as old as you feel.
—Elizabeth Arden

I refuse to admit that I am more than 52,
even if that makes my children illegitimate.
—Lady Nancy Astor

The secret of staying young is to live honestly, eat slowly,
and lie about your age.
—Lucille Ball

We grow neither better or worse as we get old, but more like ourselves.
—May L. Becker

I believe the true function of age is memory. I'm recording as fast as I can.
—Rita Mae Brown

A woman's always younger than a man of equal years.
—Elizabeth Barrett Browning

Perhaps one has to be very old before one learns to be amused
rather than shocked.
—Pearl S. Buck

Few women admit their age ... Fewer men act theirs.
—Bumper Sticker

I finally got it all together, but I forgot where I put it.
—Bumper Sticker

Every time I think that I'm getting old, and gradually going to the grave, something else happens.
—Lillian Carter

The hardest years in life are those between ten and seventy.
—Helen Hayes (at age 73)

Let me advise thee not to talk of thyself as being old. There is something in Mind Cure, after all, and if thee continually talks of thyself as being old, thee may perhaps bring on some of the infirmities of age. At least I would not risk it if I were thee.
—Hannah Whitall Smith

We are always the same age inside.
—Gertrude Stein

Living life prepares us for life, so that by the time we're too old to enjoy it, we've finally got the hang of it!
—Pamela Truax, www. AccountabilityPays.com

I will never give in to old age until I become old. And I'm not old yet!
—Tina Turner

Birthdays are good for you. The more you have, the longer you live.
—Unknown

Phew! This aging is for the birds.
—Wardene Weisser, nature photographer

With proper voice technique plus good healthy care of your body, your voice only gets better as you age.
—Joni Wilson, Voice Expert, Author "The 3-Dimensional Voice"
www.JoniWilsonVoice.com

Angels

It's not how you fly. It's how you land.
—Venna Bishop, flew as an Angel in the Crystal Cathedral for 7 years

Never drive faster than your angels can fly.
—Bumper Sticker

I've seen and met angels wearing the disguise of ordinary people
living ordinary lives.
— Tracy Chapman

Most people never have the opportunity to see an angel, or simply do not look
well enough to see them walking among us. This, however does not mean they
don't exist. Me, I'm one of the lucky few, not only have I seen an angel, I call her
my best friend.
—Lori Corkum

Be like an angel and do one small act of service for someone; be a blessing in
someone's life. We are building a bridge according to God's will and plan. Look
around your community with "Angel Eyes" filled with God's light—to see where
service is needed and know that God has sent you. Spread the positive and
uplifting light of your spirit. Open your heart and mind to your intuitive side and
feel the healing power of unconditional love that exists all around. We are here
to serve God — Just like angels.
—Jayne Howard-Feldman

Don't forget to be kind to strangers. For some who have done this have
entertained angels without realizing it.
—Hebrews 13:2

Angels do find us in our hour of need.
—Amy Huffman

Assertiveness

The basic difference between being assertive and being aggressive is how our words and behavior affect the rights and well being of others.
—Sharon Anthony Bower

A woman is like a tea bag . . . You don't know how strong she is until you put her in hot water!
—Bumper Sticker

It always cracks me up that mothers will tell their children to say "no" to their peers when they can't say "no" themselves.
—Colette Carlson, Speaker, Contributing author, "Conversations on Success"
www.colettecarlson.com

You cannot please everyone.
The sooner you get this, the better off you'll be.
—Cath Kachur, Speaker, Artist

Assertiveness is not what you do, it's who you are!
—Cal Le Mon

The most common way people give up their power is by thinking they don't have any.
—Alice Walker

No where in the human body does the effect of our emotional temperature show up faster than in our VOICE.
—Joni Wilson, Voice Expert, Author "The 3-Dimensional Voice"
www.JoniWilsonVoice.com

Attitude

Defined as:

1. Personal view of something: an opinion or general feeling about something · a positive attitude to change

2. Bodily posture: a physical posture, either conscious or unconscious, especially while interacting with others

Your attitude, feelings, or moods will infect or affect the actions, moods, and feelings of those around you. If you face the world with a cheerful expectant attitude, the world (and those in it) will know you expect more from it and will perform accordingly. If you face the world with a negative, down trodden attitude it will know you expect poor action from it and will give you those actions. Remember that the world will reflect your attitude back to you. Your attitude to the world will determine its attitude towards you (cause and effect). So one of the main rules to a successful life is to know that the world is a mirror, often a merciless mirror, of our selves and the habitual attitude we carry within us.
—Tracy Brinkmann
www.TracyBrinkmann.bizhosting.com

Don't blame me, I voted for myself!
-Iris Adam, Natural Law Party Candidate for Governor of California, 2002, 2003

Let positive thoughts warm you and illuminate you. A negative, critical person has a foot of ice around them, and no one can penetrate the surface. Positive, nurturing people have an ocean of warm water around themselves that everyone swims towards. As we all know: "It is the thought that counts." Your thoughts create your reality. Expand your personal horizons by letting go of (or at least recognize and label) your anger, fear, doubt, worry or anxiety. They hinder your capacity to experience life to the fullest. Do not only guard your thoughts, also guard your tongue.
—Adele Alfano, author "Expert Women Who Speak . . . Speak Out!," and "Life, Balance & Success Strategies by Women, for Women"

If you don't like something change it. If you can't change it, change your attitude. Don't complain.
—Maya Angelou, American poet, writer, and actress

Negative words climb into the woodwork, and into the furniture, and the next thing you know they'll be on your skin!
—Maya Angelou, American poet, writer, and actress

You've got to sing like you don't need the money.
You've got to love like you'll never get hurt.
You've got to dance like there's nobody watching.
You've got to come from the heart, if you want it to work.
—Susanna Clark

When somebody asks you, "How are you?" and you keep answering "Good, Fine, Okay, or Not-so-good," that is what is going to happen for you the rest of the day. And when you answer in a positive attitude, "Wonderful, Fabulous, Really Good, Great," life is wonderful!
—Yolanda Contreras, Supervisor, Sheraton Suites

A positive attitude can really make dreams come true — it did for me.
—Zina Garrison

Nothing in life is so hard that you can't make it easier by the way you take it.
—Ellen Glasgow

The way we live our life shows up on our face.
—Carolyn Gross, Author "Staying Calm in the Midst of Chaos"

It's not the load that breaks you down, it's the way you carry it.
—Lena Horne

The most beautiful people we have known are those who have known defeat, known suffering, known struggle, known loss, and have found their way out of the depths. These persons have an appreciation, a sensitivity, and an understanding of life that fills them with compassion, gentleness, and a deep loving concern. Beautiful people do not just happen.
—Elizabeth Kubler-Ross, Author

If you can react the same way to winning and losing, that's a big accomplishment. That quality is important because it stays with you the rest of your life, and there's going to be a life after tennis that's a lot longer than your tennis life.
—Chris Evert Lloyd, Professional Tennis Player

Could we change our attitude, we should not only see life differently, but life itself would come to be different. Life would undergo a change of appearance because we ourselves had undergone a change of attitude.
—Katherine Mansfield, Writer

A strong, positive attitude will create more miracles then any wonder drug.
—Patricia Neal

Always keep that happy attitude.
Pretend that you are holding a beautiful fragrant bouquet.
—Candice M. Pope

Adjust your daily attitude toward Happiness.
—Kay Presto, Speaker, Author "Create the Magic in YOUR Life"
Contributor to"Chicken Soup for the NASCAR Soul"

The brain is designed to protect us, not to make us successful and happy. It takes special skills to outsmart the operation of our brains and truly act by conscious choice.
—Marcia Reynolds

When we look for the bad in others, we shall surely find it.
Look for the good in others — and in yourself.
—Sheryl Roush, Speaker, Author, "Sparkle-Tudes"
Contributing Author to "The Princess Principle: Women Helping Women Discover Their Royal Spirit"
www.SparklePresentations.com

There are times when you just get down, you feel like nobody likes you. We're in high school forever. It's just what we do with it.
—Rene Russo, Actress

Don't spend time beating on a wall, hoping to transform it into a door.
—Dr. Laura Schlessinger, Radio Talk Show Personality

If you can't change your fate, change your attitude.
—Amy Tan, Actress

A healthy attitude is contagious but don't wait to catch it from others. Be a carrier.
— Unknown

Optimism is the cheerful frame of mind that enables a teakettle to sing, though in hot water up to its nose.
— Unknown

Whether a glass is half full or half empty depends on the attitude of the person looking at it.
— Unknown

I've learned from experience that the greater part of our happiness or misery depends on our dispositions and not on our circumstances.
—Martha Washington

Developing a cheerful disposition can permit an atmosphere wherein one's spirit can be nurtured and encouraged to blossom and bear fruit. Being pessimistic and negative about our experiences will not enhance the quality of our lives. A determination to be of good cheer can help us and those around us to enjoy life more fully.
—Barbara W. Winder

A Woman's Wisdom

In every girl is a goddess.
—Francesca Lia Block

Women are never what they seem to be.
There is the woman you see and there is the woman who is hidden.
Buy the gift for the woman who is hidden.
—Erma Bombeck

Let Greeks be Greeks, and women what they are.
—Anne Bradstreet

See yourself in everything because everything is already within you.
—Cynthia Brian, speaker, radio and TV show host
Author "Chicken Soup for the Gardener's Soul"
www.BeTheStarYouAre.org

The flower of a woman's wisdom blooms within her heart.
—Laurel Burch, Artist, "Celebrating the Heart of Womankind"

There is space within sisterhood for likeness and difference,
for the subtle differences that challenge and delight;
there is space for disappointment—and surprise.
—Christine Downing

Adventure is worthwhile.
—Amelia Earhart

Somewhere out in this audience may even be someone who will one day
follow in my footsteps, and preside over the White House as the president's
spouse. I wish him well.
—First lady Barbara Bush at Wellesley College 1990 commencement

Emmett's Observation: God created company so the home gets cleaned.
—Rita Emmett, Speaker, Author, "The Procrastinator's Handbook"
www.RitaEmmett.com

God gave women intuition and femininity.
Used properly, the combination easily jumbles the brain
of any man I've ever met.
—Farrah Fawcett

I used to tell my children "Do well, stay well."
Then the youngest changed it to "Be well, stay well"
and we both grew up.
—Linda Ferber

I find a woman's point of view much grander and finer than a man's.
—Katharine Hepburn

Don't compromise yourself. You are all you've got.
—Janis Joplin

Always wear expensive shoes, but try to buy them on sale.
—Erin King, Director of Kiddie Academy of Chester

A woman is the full circle.
Within her is the power to create, nurture, and transform.
—Diane Mariechild

Wisdom is not knowing what to do, it is knowing what Not to do.
--Stephanie Moles, www.TheWoman'sHeart.org

How wrong it is for a woman to expect the man to build the world she wants,
rather than to create it herself.
—Anais Nin

I am a woman above everything else.
—Jacqueline Bouvier Kennedy Onassis

Life on the planet is born of woman.
—Adrienne Rich

You gain strength, courage and confidence by every experience in which
you really stop to look fear in the face. You are able to say to yourself,
"I lived through this horror. I can take the next thing that comes along." . . .
You must do the thing you think you cannot do.
—Eleanor Roosevelt

Most women's magazines simply try to mold women
into bigger and better consumers.
—Gertrude Stein

God made man, and then he said, "I can do better than that,"
and made women.
—Adela Rogers St. Johns

Women are the architects of society.
—Harriet Beecher Stowe

If you have not the experience, ask.
There is no shame in asking, but do not pretend you know when you don't.
—Mother Teresa

Once a woman is made man's equal,
she becomes his superior.
—Margaret Thatcher

The key to understanding others is to first understand yourself.
—Unknown

Balance

Life is like riding a bike.
It is impossible to maintain your balance while standing still.
—Linda Brakeall, Author "The Respected Woman" series
www.TheRespectedWoman.com

A joyful life is a delicate balance of letting go of those things that no longer
serves us and embracing all the things that do.
—Beth Burns, Professional Life Coach
www.BrightSideCoaching.com

If your "to-do-today's" don't fit on a 3x5 card, you're too busy.
—Cath Kachur, Speaker, Artist
www.HumanTuneUp.com

There is indeed a season for every time...
Winter -- a time of quiet and clearing of the mind;
Spring -- a time of birthing the fresh vision;
Summer -- a time of sowing and nurturing the personal growth;
Autumn -- the time to enjoy and celebrate the triumphs that began
in the crisp and clear vision of winter.
We are truly the miraculous -- women with focus.
—Mona M. Mordoff, Speaker, Writer, Founder Aqua Lady Water Tenders

I believe in living fully:
       Loving,
       Laughing,
       Learning, and
       Leaving a Legacy.
—Denese Zink, University California-Irvine

Beauty

Look for the beauty in things.
—Maya Angelou

Strange that the vanity which accompanies beauty —
excusable, perhaps, when there is such great beauty,
or at any rate understandable —should persist after the beauty was gone.
—Mary Arnim

I'm not ugly, but my beauty is a total creation.
—Tyra Banks

Think of all the beauty still left around you and be happy.
—Anne Frank

I believe that children are our future.
Teach them well and let them lead the way.
Show them all the beauty they possess inside.
—Whitney Houston, Singer, Actress

Normal day, let me be aware of the treasure you are. Let me learn from you,
love you, bless you before you depart. Let me not pass you by in quest of
some rare and perfect tomorrow. Let me hold you while I may, for it may not
always be so.
—Mary Jean Iron

People are like stained glass windows — the true beauty can be seen only when
there is light from within. The darker the night, the brighter the windows.
—Elizabeth Kubler-Ross

The real sin against life is to abuse and destroy beauty, even one's own—
even more, one's own, for that has been put in our care and we are responsible
for its well-being.
—Katherine Anne Porter

Beauty is the still-birth of suffering, every woman knows that.
—Emily Prager

If you're considered a beauty, it's hard to be accepted doing anything
but standing around.
—Cybil Shepard

We know only that we are living in these bodies and have a vague idea,
because we have heard it, and because our faith tells us so, that we possess
souls. As to what good qualities there may be in our souls, or who dwells within
them, or how precious they are, those are things which seldom consider and so
we trouble little about carefully preserving the soul's beauty.
—St. Teresa of Avila

You can take no credit for beauty at sixteen.
But if you are beautiful at sixty, it will be your soul's own doing.
—Marie Carmichael Stopes

Beauty is in the eye of the beholder.
—Unknown

Practice random beauty and senseless acts of love.
—Unknown

The beauty myth moves for men as a mirage; its power lies in its ever-
receding nature. When the gap is closed, the lover embraces only his own
disillusion.
—Naomi Wolf

Behavior & Habits

You cannot make yourself feel something you do not feel,
but you can make yourself do right in spite of your feelings.
—Pearl S. Buck

The only difference between a rut and a grave is the depth.
—Bumper Sticker

A Podany Principle for how each day should start:
    A Positive Thought in your Mind
    A Smile on Your Lips
    A Feeling of Gratitude in Your Heart
—Sue Podany, Speaker, Author "Energy . . . 120 Easy Ways to Get It, Keep It,
and . . . Keep From Giving It Away!" www.SuePodany.com

Motivation is what gets you started. Habit is what keeps you going.
—Unknown

If you want to change a bad habit, cultivate a new good habit to replace it. This
is the most effective way to make positive changes in behavior.
—Diana Weiss-Wisdom, Ph.D., Author "Stress and A Healthy Ticker:
A Psychological Approach to Preventing Heart Disease"

If you're willing to do the work, you will eventually become what I call
a woman who is in full possession of herself.
—Oprah Winfrey

What gets recognized gets repeated; what gets celebrated becomes a habit.
—Leslie Yerkes, Author "Fun Works: Creating Places Where People Love to
Work," Contributor to "Business: The Ultimate Resource"
Co-author "Beans: Four Principles for Running a Business
in Good Times or Bad"

 Beliefs

It is this belief in a power larger than myself and other than myself which allows me to venture into the unknown and even the unknowable.
—Maya Angelou

"Believe that you can. Just Believe. Then trust it can be so, and take one step."
—Susan L. Gilbert, Author "The Land of I Can" and America's Focus Expert!

Desire, ask, believe, receive.
—Stella Terrill Mann

Our beliefs are like sunglasses. The color lens we look through paints our world and our experiences. If we look through shades of doom, we get gloom. If we look through shades of sparkling light, we get delight.
—Peggy O'Neill, Speaker, Author, Small Miracles Unlimited, www.YoPeggy.com

Our beliefs shape our reality – past, present and future.
Turn up the volume and listen to your thoughts carefully.
—Sheryl Roush, Author "Sparkle-Tudes!" www.SparklePresentations.com

To believe in something not yet proved and to underwrite it with our lives: it is the only way we can leave the future open.
—Lillian Smith

You can change your beliefs so they empower your dreams and desires. Create a strong belief in yourself and what you want.
—Marcia Wieder

[W]e must believe in ourselves or no one else will believe in us; we must match our aspirations with the competence, courage and determination to succeed.
—Rosalyn Sussman Yalow, US medical physicist

Business & Management

Hire the best. Pay them fairly. Communicate frequently. Provide challenges and rewards. Believe in them. Get out of their way and they'll knock your socks off.
—Mary Ann Allison

Men go to meetings to MEET. Women go to meetings to get something done!
—Cokie Roberts, interviewed in "How To Get Men To Take You Seriously In Business And In Life!" by Linda Brakeall, Author
www.LindaBrakeall.com

Leaders must develop the mindset to hunt for innovation everywhere: products, services, processes, strategies. Sustainable business futures depend on it.
—Lynda Curtin, The Opportunity Thinker

I use nothing but the best ingredients. My cookies are always baked fresh.
I price cookies so that you cannot make them at home for any less.
And I still give cookies away.
—Debbie Fields, Mrs. Field's Cookies

Power networking is being skillful not only in generating business but in enhancing your business and life for the greater good of all.
—Donna Fisher, Speaker, Author of Power Networking, and Professional Networking for Dummies
www.DonnaFisher.com   www.OnlineBusinessNetworking.com

You have to do many things yourself. Things that you cannot delegate.
—Nadine Gramling

There are so many things you can work on, so many things that you can do
in a business environment, but picking the right ones and letting other people
handle the rest is a really important lesson.
—Ann Livermore, President Business Customer Organization-Hewlett Packard
Excerpt from "Playing with the Big Boys" by Debra Pestrak
www.MostPowerfulWomen.com

Once you shape a company to service the marketplace and your services
are necessary, the company develops a compulsion of its own to grow.
—Elisabeth Claiborne Ortenberg

Never delegate to someone else, anything that you would not do yourself,
and being willing to do it first.
—Sheryl Roush, Speaker, Author "Sparkle-Tudes!"
www.SparklePresentations.com

And since when do business goals (profit) come before values, ethics,
and decency?
—Dr. Laura Schlessinger

In this jungle of business and professional ethics,
in the end it's not the lion or the tiger that will eat you alive—-
it's the mosquito! The daily decisions you make about the little things
often have the biggest impact.
—Mandi Stanley, Speaker, Author "The No-Panic Checklist for Presenters"

If you want to manage somebody, manage yourself.
Do that well and you'll be ready to stop managing.
And start leading.
—Unknown

If you want to do something well, find someone who has already "been there and done that." Then walk a bit in their shoes to get you moving in the right direction.
—Joni Wilson, Voice Expert, Author "The 3-Dimensional Business Voice"
www.JoniWilsonVoice.com

The concept of work is not static, it is fluid.
As the world changes, so do our attitudes towards our work.
We are currently at a crossroads, at the creating of yet another attitude toward work.
The new economy requires that we rethink what work is
and what work should be. If work is going to attract the best people today and retain them tomorrow, then in addition to providing the resources to live, work must also be fulfilling.
—Leslie Yerkes, Founder and President, Catalyst Consulting Group, Inc.
Co-author "301 Ways to Have Fun at Work"
Author "Fun Works: Creating Places Where People Love to Work"
Contributor to "Business: The Ultimate Resource"
Co-author "Beans: Four Principles for Running a Business
in Good Times or Bad"

Careers

When people go to work, they shouldn't have to leave their hearts at home.
—Betty Bender

Meeting - an event at which the minutes are kept and the hours are lost.
—Bumper Sticker

I fight poverty, I work.
—Bumper Sticker

Don't consider your wastebasket to be an enemy who gobbles up your important data; consider it to be a friend who must be nurtured and fed.
—Rita Emmett, Speaker, Author The Procrastinator's Handbook
www.RitaEmmett.com

You have to know exactly what you want out of your career.
If you want to be a star, you don't bother with other things.
—Marilyn Horne

You really have to take charge of your own career.
Nobody is going to do that for you.
—Darlene Kerr, Executive Vice President - Niagara Mohawk
Excerpt from "Playing with the Big Boys" by Debra Pestrak
www.MostPowerfulWomen.com

Getting ahead in a difficult profession requires avid faith in yourself. You must be able to sustain yourself against staggering blows. There is no code of conduct to help beginners. That is why some people with mediocre talent, but with great inner drive, go much further than people with vastly superior talent.
—Sophia Loren

Love what you do for a living . . . and live what you love.
—Maria Marsala, www.ElevatingYou.com

A job is what you do for a paycheck.
Work is what you do for a life.
—Eileen McDargh, Speaker, Author of "Work for a Living & Still Be Free to Live,"
and "The Resilient Spirit"
www.TheResilientSpirit.com

When you leave work, leave it!
—Carolyn Montez, School Administrative Assistant
Los Angeles Unified School District

The phrase "working mother" is redundant.
—Jane Sellman

Don't sacrifice your life to work and ideals.
The most important things in life are human relations.
I found that out too late.
—Katharinde Susannah Prichard, Australian Author

The person who knows HOW will always have a job.
The person who knows WHY will always be his boss.
—Diane Ravitch

I have yet to hear a man ask for advice on how to combine marriage
and a career.
—Gloria Steinem

Career change is a process and not an event.
Transforming what you do will not happen overnight.
Career change represents personal growth, not career failure.
—Anne Wilkins, Evergreen Coaching, Inc.

The integration of fun and work isn't about what you do,
it's about who you're being when you're doing your work.
—Leslie Yerkes, Co-author "301 Ways to Have Fun at Work"
Author "Fun Works: Creating Places Where People Love to Work"

Cats

Creation According to Cats
On the 1st day, Goddess created the cat.
On the 2nd day, Goddess created man to serve the cat.
On the 3rd day, Goddess created all the animals of the earth
        to serve as potential food for the cat.
On the 4th day, Goddess created honest toil so that man
        could labor for the good of the cat.
On the 5th day, Goddess created the sparkle ball so that the cat
        might or might not play with it.
On the 6th day Goddess created veterinary science
        to keep the cat healthy and the man broke.
On the 7th day, Goddess tried to rest, but She had to scoop the litterbox.
—Submitted by Teri L. Milligan

Language of Cats
Catitude — an air of self-confidence that exudes
"I was created to be worshiped, and you'd better not forget it!"
Meowvelous — a cut above "marvelous."
Pussonality — feline personality traits. (Example: Catitude)
Purrfect — a cut above "perfect."
—Gail Rossi, Gallery Owner, Cat Alley   >^..^<
www.CatAlley.net

Things I Learned about Love from My Cat
1. Always be ready to play.
2. When you are happy to see someone, stretch your arms up
    to them and ask to be picked up.
3. If the person you love forgets to feed you dinner, don't take it personally.
4. Talk to the one you love, incessantly and constantly.
5. Don't be afraid to ask to be touched.
6. Show your love and adoration by bringing presents.
7. Purr when the person you love is anywhere near you.
8. Encourage the person you love to take naps with you.
9. Always comfort the person you love, regardless of whether they need
    emotional or physical comfort.
—Unknown

In the middle of a world that has always been a bit mad, the cat walks with confidence.
—Roseanne Anderson

As every cat owner knows, nobody owns a cat.
—Ellen Perry Berkeley

Dogs come when they're called; cats take a message and get back to you later.
—Mary Bly

Cats always seem so very wise, when staring with their half-closed eyes.
Can they be thinking, "I'll be nice, and maybe she will feed me twice?"
—Bette Midler

If you want a kitten, start out by asking for a horse.
—Naomi, age 15, "Advice from Kids"

People that hate cats will come back as mice in their next life.
—Faith Resnick

Dogs have masters.
Cats have staff.
—Unknown

Dogs believe they are human.
Cats believe they are God.
—Unknown

No one can have experienced to the fullest the true sense of achievement and satisfaction who have never pursued and successfully caught his tail.
—Rosalind Welcher

Challenges

Bouncing Back from Life's Setbacks

Create an action plan that will move you through the madness and bounce back from the rough roads that lie ahead.

1. Reinforce The Belief In Yourself
2. Assess The Impact Of Your Crisis
3. Understand What You Can And Cannot Control
4. Call On Your Inner Strength
5. Talk To Others
6. Don't Lose Your Sense Of Humor
7. Bounce Back
—Carole Copeland Thomas, MBA
www.TellCarole.com

An obstacle is an opportunity not yet recognized.
—Perry A, Author "People Are Just Desserts"
www.PerryA.com

I wanted to be scared again . . . I wanted to feel unsure again.
That's the only way I learn, the only way I feel challenged.
—Connie Chung

I've often thought that when something is hard for you, whether it's going to law school or anything else that challenges you, that's probably what you should do.
—Hillary Rodham Clinton

No human being is immune to adversity or personal setbacks.
—Hillary Rodham Clinton

There are no laurels in life . . . just new challenges.
—Katharine Hepburn

For a long time it seemed to me that real life was about to begin, but there was always some obstacle in the way. Something had to be got through first, some unfinished business; time still to be served, a debt to be paid. Then life would begin. At last it dawned on me that these obstacles were my life.
—Bette Howland

To fly we have to have resistance.
—Maya Lin

Obstacles are those frightful things you see
when you take your eyes off your goal.
—Hannah More

If we do not rise to the challenge of our unique capacity to shape our lives,
to seek the kinds of growth that we find individually fulfilling, then we can have
no security: we will live in a world of sham, in which our selves are determined
by the will of others, in which we will be constantly buffeted and increasingly
isolated by the changes round us.
—Nena O'Neil

Pain is not a punishment. Pain is a gift. It's an invitation to GROW.
Our difficulties in life call us to go deeper within ourselves.
Our challenges force us to develop better skills, more abilities,
and new ways of thinking, doing and being.
They draw forth a greater strength and deeper wisdom
from our inner selves.
—Peggy O'Neill, Speaker, Author "Walking Tall:Overcoming Inner Smallness
No Matter What Size You Are"
Small Miracles Unlimited, www.YoPeggy.com

If you want the rainbow, you gotta put up with the rain.
—Dolly Parton

The bigger the project, the bigger the goal,
the bigger the challenges you will face.
Knowing that allows us not be surprised or upset when they come your way.
Then we can take the next step forward more quickly.
—Debra Pestrak, Speaker, Author
www.DebraPestrak.com

Face a challenge and find joy in the capacity to meet it.
—Ayn Rand

Life's challenges are not supposed to paralyze you,
they're supposed to help you discover who you are.
—Bernice Johnson Reagon

You have to erect a fence and say, "Okay, scale this."
—Linda Ronstadt

Every time you meet a situation, though you think at the moment it is
an impossibility and you go through the tortures of the damned,
once you have met it and lived through it you find that forever after
you are freer than you were before.
—Eleanor Roosevelt

It doesn't matter what you're trying to accomplish.
It's all a matter of discipline.
I was determined to discover what life held for me
beyond the inner-city streets.
—Wilma Rudolph, 1940-1994, Olympic Gold Medallist in Track

Sometimes the challenge is the view from which we see the challenge.
If you can't handle the little stuff, you may never get to the big stuff.
--Heshie Segal, Speaker, Founder-The Girlfriend Connection
www.JetNettingConnection.com

To be tested is good. The challenged life may be the best therapist.
—Gail Sheehy

When people keep telling you that you can't do a thing,
you kind of like to try it.
—Margaret Chase Smith

There is nothing that you can say
that is so bad or hurtful that I can't get over.
—Rozelia K. Spikes, Speaker, Philosopher
Author, "Understanding the Power of Women: Words to Live By",
and "Reflections"
www.rkspikes.com

Least favorite word: "Impossible"
—Barbra Streisand, interviewed on Screen Actor's Guild

Challenges make you discover things about yourself
that you never really knew.
—Cicely Tyson

After all it is those who have a deep and real inner life
who are best able to deal with the irritating details of outer life.
—Evelyn Underhill

Always continue the climb.
It is possible for you to do whatever you choose,
if you first get to know who you are and are willing to work
with a power that is greater than ourselves to do it.
—Oprah Winfrey

Change

Seek not to change the world, but choose to change your mind about the world.
—A Course in Miracles

Life is not rejection, but it is constantly in the flow of re-direction.
We sometimes call it change. Keep the flow going.
—Perry A, Author "People Are Just Desserts"
www.PerryA.com

Who we are never changes. Who we think we are does.
—Mary S. Almanac

That's the risk you take if you change: that people you've been involved with won't like the new you. But other people who do will come along.
—Lisa Alther

Only I can change my life. No one can do it for me.
—Carol Burnett

If you don't like something change it;
if you can't change it, change the way you think about it.
—Mary Engelbreit

To keep our faces toward change, and behave like free spirits
in the presence of fate, is strength undefeatable.
—Helen Keller

I'm always reminding people that the one constant you can count on is that things happen – and usually when you're not in the mood for them.
—Loretta LaRoche, Author "Relax-You May Only Have a Few Minutes Left"

A stitch in time saves nine—- but NOT if you've outgrown the pants.
—Eileen McDargh, Speaker, Author "Off the Chart Results, An Anthology of Advice from Experts" www.EileenMcDargh.com

Never doubt that a small group of thoughtful,
committed citizens can change the world.
Indeed, it's the only thing that ever has.
—Margaret Mead

None of us knows what the next change is going to be,
what unexpected opportunity is just around the corner,
waiting to change all the tenor of our lives.
—Kathleen Norris, writer

Life will never the be same. Life is always changing. Embrace it.
—Debra Pestrak, Speaker, Author
www.DebraPestrak.com

Some people change their ways when they see the light,
others when they feel the heat.
—Caroline Schoeder

Change can either challenge or threaten us.
Your beliefs pave your way to success or block you.
—Marsha Sinetar

A woman may be able to change the world,
but she will never be able to change a man.
—Amy Snowden

Though I might travel afar, I will meet only what I carry with me,
for every man is a mirror. We see only ourselves reflected in those around us.
Their attitudes and actions are only a reflection of our own. The whole world
and its condition has its counter parts within us all. Turn the gaze inward.
Correct yourself and your world will change.
—Kirsten Zambucka

Character

All struggles begin with me. Struggle is an inside job.
—Perry A., Author "People Are Just Desserts" www.PerryA.com

To succeed is nothing; it's an accident. But to feel no doubts about oneself is something very different; it is character.
—Louisa May Alcott

Character contributes to beauty. It fortifies a woman as her youth fades.
—Jacqueline Bisset

Parents can only give good advice or put [their children] on the right paths, but the final forming of a person's character lies in their own hands.
—Anne Frank

Courage is the ladder on which all the other virtues mount.
—Clare Booth Luce

When you have decided what you believe, what you feel must be done, have the courage to stand alone and be counted.
—Eleanor Roosevelt

Integrity isn't lost in one fell swoop. No one wakes up one morning and says, "I think I'll embezzle $150,000 today." Integrity is lost a little bit at a time.
—Catherine Tucek

"Please God, I've got enough character today . . ."
—Oprah Winfrey (upon waking one morning)

Childhood

But childhood prolonged, cannot remain a fairyland.
It becomes a hell.
—Louise Bogan

We say that a girl with her doll anticipates the mother.
It is more true, perhaps, that most mothers are still but children with playthings.
—Francis H. Bradley

Never help a child with a task at which he feels he can succeed.
—Judy Garland

Stories fill our lives as children,
They help us learn to imagine and dream of possibilities,
To believe in possibilities is to create a limitless future,
To create a limitless future is to realize the brilliance within.
—Marian Madonia, Speaker, www.MarianMotivates.com

Let a man turn to his own childhood — no further —
if he will renew his sense of remoteness, and of the mystery of change.
—Alice Meynell

I think, at a child's birth, if a mother could ask a fairy godmother to endow it
with the most useful gift, that gift would be curiosity.
—Eleanor Roosevelt

Children are the sum of what mothers contribute to their lives.
—Unknown

That great Cathedral space which was childhood.
—Virginia Woolf

Children

Children are like flowers, nurture them and they will grow up
strong and beautiful.
—Lydia Boyd, Past International Director, Toastmasters International

Children are God's most natural method of birth control.
—Linda Brakeall, Author "How To Get Men to Take You Seriously
in Business and in LIFE!"

I may be the only mother in America who knows exactly
what their child is up to all the time.
—Barbara Bush

Walk with me in the sand. One thousand steps. Ten thousand words.
One indelible memory to share forever.
--Connie Hope Diamond

Dear God,
Thank you for the baby brother but what I asked for was a puppy.
I never asked for anything before. You can look it up.
—Joyce (Kid's Theology)

Babies are necessary to grown-ups. A new baby is like the beginning of all
things —wonder, hope, a dream of possibilities. In a world that is cutting down
its trees to build highways, losing its earth to concrete . . . babies are almost the
only remaining link with nature, with the natural world of living things from
which we spring.
—Eda J. Le Shan

Human beings are the only creatures that allow their children
to come back home.
—Patty Paul

The carefree laughter of children playing outside my office window this morning is not a distraction; it is a joy. It also reminds me that we should keep that same uninhibited joy in our adult lives.
—Kay Presto, Speaker, Author "Create the Magic in YOUR Life"

I always had three rules when raising my daughter . . .
1) to know her friends well;
2) to choose battles wisely;
3) to treat her with respect.
—Debra Simpson, www.DebraSimpson.com

Parents learn a lot from their children about coping with life.
—Muriel Spark

For one mother, joy is the quiet pleasure found in gently rubbing shampoo into her young child's hair. For another woman it's taking a long walk alone, while for yet another it's reliving in a much — anticipated vacation.
—Eileen Stukane

Teenagers and Cats - Any Similarities?

1. Neither teenagers nor cats turn their heads when you call them by name.
2. No matter what you do for them, it is not enough. Indeed, all humane efforts are barely adequate to compensate for the privilege of waiting on them hand and foot.
3. You rarely see a cat walking outside of the house with an adult human being, and it can be safely said that no teenager in his or her right mind wants to be seen in public with his or her parents.
4. Even if you tell jokes as well as Jay Leno, neither your cat nor your teen will ever crack a smile.
5. No cat or teenager shares your taste in music.
6. Cats and teenagers can lie on the living-room sofa for hours on end without moving, barely breathing.
7. Cats have nine lives. Teenagers carry on as if they did.
8. Cats and teenagers yawn in exactly the same manner, communicating that ultimate human ecstasy... a sense of complete and utter boredom.
9. Cats and teenagers do not improve anyone's furniture.
10. Cats that are free to roam outside sometimes have been known to return in the middle of the night to deposit a dead animal in your bedroom. Teenagers are not above that sort of behavior.

Want to know how to raise teens, then? Keep and read regularly a guidebook on cats! Plus, keep plenty of food out, and make no sudden moves! They'll respond with affection for you sooner or later, and it will be marvelous!

Chocolate

It's not that chocolates are a substitute for love.
Love is a substitute for chocolate.
Chocolate is, let's face it, far more reliable than a man.
—Miranda Ingram

Chocolate causes certain endocrine glands to secrete hormones that affect your feelings and behavior by making you happy. Therefore, it counteracts depression, in turn reducing the stress of depression. Your stress-free life helps you maintain a youthful disposition, both physically and mentally. So, eat lots of chocolate!
—Elaine Sherman, Author "Book of Divine Indulgences"

I never met a chocolate I didn't like.
—Deanna Troi, in Star Trek: The Next Generation, TV Series

Chocolate is cheaper than therapy and you don't need an appointment.
—Unknown

There are four basic food groups:
1)milk chocolate
2)dark chocolate
3)white chocolate, and
4)chocolate truffles.
—Unknown

All I really need is love, but a little chocolate now and then doesn't hurt!
—Lucy Van Pelt (in Peanuts cartoon)

Strength is the capacity to break a chocolate bar into four pieces with your bare hands - and then eat just one of the pieces.
—Judith Viorst

Choices

When you make choices with you in mind, you have no regrets.
—Patrice Baker, Speaker, www.PowerOfWords.com

Life is about our choices. Choices change lives.
—Cynthia Brian, speaker, radio and TV show host
Author "Chicken Soup for the Gardener's Soul", www.bethestaryouare.org

The choices you make in life tell your life's story.
—Cathy Cabell, Metro National, Director of Residential Properties

I give people enough rope — they either hang themselves or make macrame.
—Linnda Durre', Ph.D., Dreams Come True Enterprises, LLC

It's all about choices and having a positive outlook.
Even if you fail, you always learn something through the process.
—Karen Garrison, President, Pitney-Bowes Management Services
Excerpt from interview "Playing with the Big Boys" by Debra Pestrak
www.MostPowerfulWomen.com

Make the choice to be your highest and best self,
regardless of the circumstances.
—Rosalene Glickman, Ph.D.,Author, Optimal Thinking

Every day we make choices, decisions about what and how our life will be.
Each day we go forward or backwards in getting what we want in life.
Sometimes we don't make the right choices, but we make the choice we
thought best at the moment. We all make mistakes. It's learning from our
mistakes and letting them go that determines our future.
—Debra Pestrak, Speaker, Author, www.DebraPestrak.com

One's philosophy is not best expressed in words; it is expressed in the choices one makes. In the long run, we shape our lives and we shape ourselves. The process never ends until we die. And, the choices we make are ultimately our own responsibility.
—Eleanor Roosevelt, 1884-1962, Former American First Lady

Choice - your greatest power.
—Aleta Pippin, abstract painter and entrepreneur, A. Pippin's Art with Heart
Author - "Yikes! My Butt's Falling . . . Humorous 'Tails' of Baby Boomers Searching for the Meaning of Life"

The more responsibility you take for that which occurs in your life, the more power you have. Love your life, live powerfully.
—Laura Rubinstein, Coach, Hypnotherapist
www.LBRandAssociates.com

In this jungle of business and professional ethics, in the end it's not the lion or the tiger that will eat you alive—-it's the mosquito! The daily decisions you make about the little things often have the biggest impact.
—Mandi Stanley, Speaker, Author, "The No-Panic Checklist for Presenters"

It is not a question of need or want... but only being out of them.s
(Oreo cookies)!
—Bonnie Weisser

The world is terrified by joyful women. Take a stand—be one anyway!
—Marianne Williamson, "Author A Woman's Worth"

Church Notices

These sentences actually appeared in printed church bulletins
or were announced in church services:

Bertha Belch, a missionary from Africa, will be speaking tonight at Calvary
Methodist. Come hear Bertha Belch all the way from Africa.

Announcement in a church bulletin for a national PRAYER & FASTING
Conference: "The cost for attending the Fasting and Prayer conference
includes meals."

The sermon this morning: "Jesus Walks on the Water."

The sermon tonight: "Searching for Jesus."

"Ladies, don't forget the rummage sale. It's a chance to get rid of those things
not worth keeping around the house. Don't forget your husbands."

The peacemaking meeting scheduled for today has been cancelled
due to a conflict.

Remember in prayer the many who are sick of our community.

Don't let worry kill you off - let the Church help.

Miss Charlene Mason sang "I will not pass this way again,"
giving obvious pleasure to the congregation.

For those of you who have children and don't know it,
we have a nursery downstairs.

Next Thursday there will be tryouts for the choir.
They need all the help they can get.

Barbara remains in the hospital and needs blood donors for more transfusions.
She is also having trouble sleeping and requests tapes of Pastor Jack's sermons.

During the absence of our Pastor, we enjoyed the rare privilege of hearing a
good sermon when J.F. Stubbs supplied our pulpit.

Irving Benson and Jessie Carter were married on October 24 in the church.
So ends a friendship that began in their school days.

At the evening service tonight, the sermon topic will be "What is Hell?"
Come early and listen to our choir practice.

Eight new choir robes are currently needed, due to the addition of several
new members and to the deterioration of some older ones.

The Lutheran men's group will meet at 6:00 PM. Steak, mashed potatoes,
green beans, bread and dessert will be served for a nominal feel.

Please place your donation in the envelope along with the deceased person
you want remembered.

Attend and you will hear an excellent speaker and heave a healthy lunch.

The church will host an evening of fine dining, superb entertainment,
and gracious hostility.

Potluck supper Sunday at 5:00 PM - prayer and medication to follow.

The ladies of the Church have cast off clothing of every kind.
They may be seen in the basement on Friday afternoon.

This evening at 7:00 PM there will be a hymn sing in the park across
from the Church. Bring a blanket and come prepared to sin.

Ladies Bible Study will be held Thursday morning at 10.
All ladies are invited to lunch in the Fellowship Hall after the B.S. is done.

The pastor would appreciate it if the ladies of the congregation would
lend him their electric girdles for the pancake breakfast next Sunday.

Low Self-Esteem Support Group will meet Thursday at 7:00 PM.
Please use the back door.

The eighth-graders will be presenting Shakespeare's Hamlet in the Church
basement Friday at 7:00 PM. The Congregation is invited to attend this tragedy.

Weight Watchers will meet at 7:00 PM at the First Presbyterian Church.

Please use large double door at the side entrance.

Common Sense

Common sense is perhaps the most equally divided,
but surely the most underemployed, talent in the world.
—Christine Collange

That's the way things come clear. All of a sudden.
And then you realize how obvious they've been all along.
—Madeline L'Engle

Happiness for the average person may be said to flow largely from common
sense — adapting one-self to circumstances — and a sense of humor.
—Beatrice Lillie

Turn you mind off and look again. You will see it.
--Stephanie Moles, Founder of The Woman's Heart
www.TheWoman'sHeart.org

Falling in love consists merely in uncorking the imagination
and bottling the common sense.
—Helen Rowland

It makes sense that there is no sense without God.
—Edith Schaeffer

Everybody gets so much information all day long that they
lose their common sense.
—Gertrude Stein

Everyone is smart at something; I just need to find what it is.
—Bonnie Weisser

Communication

Anyone can say it in a thousand words . . .
Now, say it in one.
—Cynthia Berger

When was the last time you told someone that you appreciate them —
because you really do?
—Lydia Boyd, Past International Director, Toastmasters International

When you tell someone that they are ugly, stupid or crazy, it will make
them feel ugly, stupid and crazy. When you tell people that you appreciate,
respect and love them, it will make them feel appreciated, respected and loved
enabling them to create a safer, healthier and more prosperous community,
country and world.
—Helice "the Spark" Bridges, Author "Who I Makes A Difference"
Founder and President, Difference Makers International

Dance is the hidden language of the soul, of the body.
—Martha Graham, US dancer, choreographer

We have to ask for what we want, or we won't get it.
If we don't ask for what we want, we can't be surprised when we don't get it.
We might ask for what we want and not get it, but if we don't ask,
we almost certainly won't get it.
—Kathelen R. Johnson
www.TheTeachersVoice.com

Enthusiasm turns "I have to" into "I want to"
and "I don't want to" into "I'm doing it anyway"
and "It's not fun" into "I'll make this fun."
—Mary Marcdante, Speaker, Author "Living with Enthusiasm:
How the 21-Day Smile Diet Can Change Your Life"
www.MaryMarcdante.com

Until you say No, you have said Yes.
--Stephanie Moles, Founder of The Woman's Heart
www.TheWoman'sHeart.org

The most important words you will ever hear are the words you say to yourself.
—Mona M. Moon, Speaker
www.MonaMoon.com

How we communicate with ourselves and others will determine our success.
—Debra Pestrak, Speaker, Author "Playing with the Big Boys"
www.DebraPestrak.com

There's not enough appreciation in the world today.
That's why I send a lot of thank you notes and handwritten messages.
We all ought to be more kind to each other.
—Julia Roush

The most brilliant revelation I've had in communication and
understanding others (particularly men) was reading Deborah Tannen's
books including *Talking From 9 to 5*, that women nod our heads when
we are in agreement; whereas men nod when they are listening —
not necessarily agreeing! That explains SO much!
—Sheryl Roush, Speaker, Author
www.SparklePresentations.com

Language is our way of communicating what we want and who we are.
By using bad language, we diminish the divine spark within us that defines
our humanity.
—Dr. Laura Schlessinger

Improve your listening skills and watch your credibility increase.
—Jennifer Rousseau Sedlock
www.JenniferSpeaks.com

The quality of your writing directly reflects the quality of your work.
—Mandi Stanley, Speaker, Author "The No-Panic Checklist for Presenters"UNDERSTANDING does not necessarily mean AGREEMENT.
— Unknown

As a speaker on business communication, one of the things I often say is "Communication technology keeps getting in the way of Communication."
—Helen Wilkie, Speaker, Author "Message Received and Understood!"
www.MHWCom.com

The voice has no brain and only believes what you believe.
Watch your words as well as your beliefs.
—Joni Wilson, Voice Expert, Author "The 3-Dimensional Voice"
www.JoniWilsonVoice.com

Attempting to communicate without connecting first
is like speaking into a telephone without a dial tone.
We know we said everything clearly
but somehow the message didn't get through.
—Pamela Ziemann, Speaker
www.PamelaZiemann.com

Compliments

When you put someone down, they feel down. When you build someone up, they rise to the level of their innate greatness.
—Helice "the Spark" Bridges, Author "Who I Am Makes A Difference"
Founder and President, Difference Makers International

Accepting what others see as your strengths is crucial to your continued growth. Compliments are a gift. They are an opportunity for you and another person to connect in a powerful, positive way. How did you handle the last compliment directed at you? Did you accept it?
—Rhonda Britten, Speaker, Author "Fearless Living: Live Without Excuses and Love Without Regret"

You can never over acknowledge as long as your acknowledgment is sincere, comes from the heart, and is given as a gift.
—Donna Fisher, Speaker, Author "People Power"
www.DonnaFisher.com

We need 4 hugs a day for survival. We need 8 hugs a day for maintenance. We need 12 hugs a day for growth.
—Virginia Satir

A word of encouragement during a failure
is worth more than an hour of praise after success.
—Unknown

Confidence

Toot your own horn loud and clear to help others gain by your expertise.
—Debbie Allen, Speaker, Author "Confessions of Shameless Self Promoters"
www.DebbieAllen.com

Life is not easy for any of us. But what of that? We must have perseverance
and above all confidence in ourselves. We must believe that we are gifted for
something and that this thing must be attained.
—Marie Curie, Polish-French chemist

Chain-complaining only leads to your own private pity pit. You've got to erect a
ladder right out of that pit by changing your vocabulary from pain to power.
—Judith Parker Harris, Speaker, Author "Move from Blocked to Block-Buster"

Class is an aura of confidence that is being sure without being cocky.
Class has nothing to do with money. Class never runs scared.
It is self-discipline and self-knowledge. It's the sure footedness that
comes with having proved you can meet life.
—Ann Landers

You've got to take the initiative and play your game.
In a decisive set, confidence is the difference.
—Chris Evert Lloyd, Professional Tennis Player

She lacks confidence, she craves admiration insatiably.
She lives on the reflections of herself in the eyes of others.
She does not care to be herself.
—Anais Nin

You gain strength, experience and confidence by every experience where you really stop to look fear in the face. You must do the thing you cannot do.
—Eleanor Roosevelt

Why have opinions if you're not going to feel strongly about them?
—Sheryl Roush, Speaker, Author

You may have to fight a battle more than once to win it.
—Margaret Thatcher

NEVER WASTE an ENTRANCE or EXIT!
—Cathi Watson, Speaker, Author, Radio and TV host/producer
www.ageless4life.com

Self confidence is the key to the universe.
—Carrol Wrackley

Confidence and courage come through preparation and practice.
—Unknown

Confidence is the feeling you have before you understand the situation.
—Unknown

Cooperation & Teamwork

The secrets to success lie not in what you do but in how you do it
and how well you work with others along the way.
—Donna Fisher, Speaker, Author "Power Networking"
www.DonnaFisher.com, www.OnlineBusinessNetworking.com

I suppose leadership at one time meant muscles,
but today it means getting along with people.
—Indira Gandhi

No matter what accomplishments you make, somebody helped you.
—Althea Gibson

Understanding people—what's on their minds, what it takes to engage them
in an idea and position them to be willing to work with you—is a critical skill.
—Jean Hamilton, CEO, Prudential Insurance Company of America
Excerpt from interview "Playing with the Big Boys" by Debra Pestrak
www.MostPowerfulWomen.com

Teamwork is the ability to work together toward a common vision.
The ability to direct individual accomplishment toward organizational
objectives. It is the fuel that allows common people to attain uncommon
results.
—Charlotte Lunsford

Win together, lose together, play together, stay together.
—Debra Mancuso

Just remember the Titanic was build by professionals,
The ark was built by volunteers.
—Unknown

Count Your Blessings

It's a Matter of Perspective

If you woke up this morning with more health than illness . . .
you are more blessed than the million who will not survive this week.

If you have never experienced the danger of battle, the loneliness of
imprisonment, the agony of torture, or the pangs of starvation . . .
you are ahead of 500 million people in the world.

If you can attend a church meeting without fear of harassment, arrest, torture,
or death . . . you are more blessed than three billion people in the world.

If you have food in the refrigerator, clothes on your back, a roof overhead
and a place to sleep . . . you are richer than 75% of this world.

If you have money in the bank, in your wallet, and spare change in a dish
someplace . . . you are among the top 8% of the world's wealthy.

If your parents are still alive and still married . . . you are very rare, even in the
United States.

If you hold up your head with a smile on your face and are truly thankful . . .
you are blessed because the majority can, but most do not.

If you can hold someone's hand, hug them or even touch them on the
shoulder..you are blessed because you can offer God's healing touch.

If you prayed yesterday and today . . . you are in the minority because you
believe God does hear and answer prayers.

If you can read this message, you are more blessed than over two billion people
in the world that cannot read at all.

Have a good day, count your blessings.

— Author Unknown

Courage

Do the right thing and deal with the results.
—Caroline Alberti, University California-Irvine, Police

The ability to realize when we were wrong - and to correct the problem - is one of the most important skills we can master as we move into the new century.
—Natalie Angier

I'm not funny. What I am is brave.
—Lucille Ball

Courage is fear that has said its prayers.
—Dorothy Bernard

It takes a lot of courage to show your dreams to someone else.
—Erma Bombeck

Waking up to the wonder of you, knowing that you are absolutely enough, embracing who you are fully and completely, relishing your life: that is fearless living.
—Rhonda Britten, Founder of the Fearless Living Institute
Author "Fearless Loving: 8 Simple Truths That Will Change the Way You Date, Mate and Relate"

Give me such courage and I can scale the hardest peaks alone, and transform every stumbling block into a stepping stone.
—Gail Brook Burket

We need to find the courage to say NO to the things and people that are not serving us if we want to rediscover ourselves and live our lives with authenticity.
—Barbara De Angelis

Courage is like a muscle. We strengthen it with use.
—Ruth Gordon

One life is all we have and we live it as we believe in living it.
And then it is gone. But to sacrifice what you are and live without belief, that's more terrible than dying.
—Joan of Arc

When you have decided what you believe, what you feel must be done, have the courage to stand alone and be counted.
—Eleanor Roosevelt

Courage is sticking to your values when you know others in your circumstances are straying to get ahead.
--Heshie Segal, Speaker, Founder-The Girlfriend Connection
www.JetNettingConnection.com

Having courage does not mean we feel no fear; it means acting despite fear in the most effective way we can.
—Marsha Sinetar

The only courage people need – is the courage to live their own dreams.
—Oprah Winfrey

. . . The true meaning of courage is to be afraid, and then, with your knees knocking and your heart racing, to step out of the way – even when that step makes sense to nobody but you.
—Oprah Winfrey

Creativity & Imagination

Creativity is a God-given ability to take something ordinary and make it into something special. The creative spirit is part of our heritage as children of the One who created all things. Nurturing our creativity is part of our responsibility as stewards of God's good gifts.
—Emilie Barnes
Women's Devotional Bible 2, New International Version

Imagination has always had powers of resurrection that no science can match.
—Ingrid Bengis

I want to create images that remind us of our connectedness to our inner selves and to each other. I listen to my heart and it tells me to dream.
As I dream I create.
—Laurel Burch, Artist, "Celebrating the Heart of Womankind"

When the imagination and will power are in conflict, are antagonistic, it is always the imagination which wins, without any exception.
—Emile Coué

We cast away priceless time in dreams, born of imagination, fed upon illusion and put to death by reality.
—Judy Garland

Creativity lies within the imagination, and action brings it into reality.
—Susan L. Gilbert, Author "The Land of I Can" and America's Focus Expert!

Ideas move fast when their time comes.
—Carolyn Heilbrun

I got something done, because I didn't know it couldn't be done.
—Blanche Katz, MSN, RN, CS, GN , Speaker, Gerontological Educator

Stories fill our lives as children,
They help us learn to imagine and dream of possibilities,
To believe in possibilities is to create a limitless future,
To create a limitless future is to realize the brilliance within.
—Marian Madonia, Speaker, www.MarianMotivates.com

A #2 pencil and a dream can take you anywhere.
—Joyce A. Myers

All my concerts had no sounds in them; they were completely silent.
People had to make up their own music in their minds!
—Yoko Ono

To imagine the unimaginable is the highest use of the imagination.
—Cynthia Ozick, Novelist, Short-story writer

A great idea is usually original to more than one discoverer.
Great ideas come when the world needs them.
Great ideas surround the world's ignorance and press for admission.
—Elizabeth Stuart Phelps

The imagination equips us to perceive reality when it is not fully materialized.
—Mary Caroline Richards

When you think something, you think in picture. You don't think a thought in
words. You think a picture that expresses your thought. Working with this
picture will produce it into your experience.
—Grace Speare

By visualizing your goals, you can get your subconscious to work toward
making these mental pictures come true.
—*Success* Magazine

What you hold in your imagination about yourself, you will become.
- Unknown

Customer Service

Customer Service is like a diamond. To be perfect, it needs to be flawless.
—Eln Albert, Speaker, Author

We treat our people like royalty.
If you honor and serve the people who work for you,
they will honor and serve you.
—Mary Kay Ash, Founder Mary Kay Cosmetics

We don't want to push our ideas on to customers,
we simply want to make what they want.
—Laura Ashley

Make a customer, not a sale.
—Katherine Barchetti

If you don't care, your customer never will.
—Marlene Blaszczyk

The client doesn't care about all the other clients you have—and shouldn't have
to. But when you are communicating with a client, you must convey to that
client that you appreciate the personal importance of the case (or relationship)
to the client and treat that person's case (or account) with the seriousness the
client him or herself holds.
—Elise Dee Beraru, Attorney

Enthusiasm is the ability to show someone such a strong level of passion, interest, and concern for a person, situation, or product that even in difficult situations people give you the benefit of the doubt, do business with you again, and refer you to your friends.
—Mary Marcdante, Speaker, Author "Living with Enthusiasm: How the 21-Day Smile Diet Can Change Your Life"
www.MaryMarcdante.com

Always think of your customers as suppliers first. Work closely with them, so they can supply you with the information you need to supply them with the right products and services.
—Susan Marthaller

The customer is our reason for being here.
—Unknown

The customer is the final inspector.
—Unknown

Revolve your world around the customer
and more customers will revolve around you.
—Heather Williams

 Dance

I always thought that if I learned to stand on my own two feet I could dance through life. It's true.
—Natalie D. Brecher, CPM®, Speaker, Author of "Business without Biceps: The Untold Truths of Women in Business and How to Make Them Work for You"

The truest expression of a people is in its dances and its music . . .
Bodies never lie.
—Agnes De Mille

Everybody can dance. Our feet will follow our heart much better than the head!
—Terry Freeman-Sweeney, Aerobic, Dance, Pilates, Yoga instructor

We look at the dance to impart the sensation of living in an affirmation of life, to energize the spectator into keener awareness of the vigor, the mystery, the humor, the variety, and the wonder of life.
—Martha Graham, US dancer, choreographer

Nobody cares if you can't dance well. Just get up and dance.
Great dancers are not great because of their technique, they are great because of their passion.
—Martha Graham, US dancer, choreographer

Music enriches the ears of our body, then moves our body to dance, which avails the spirit to live.
—Mona M. Mordoff, Speaker, Writer

We must be steady enough in ourselves, to be open and to let the winds of life blow through us, to be our breath, our inspiration; to breathe with them, mobile and soft in the limberness of our bodies, in our agility, our ability, as it were, to dance, and yet to stand upright . . .
—Mary Caroline Richards

When some men dance they're all feet, and when they stop they're all hands.
—Unknown

In dancing, the women usually know the steps and the men know the holds.
—Unknown

Only the wise can dance the rhythm of life.
—Unknown

Anyone who thinks sunshine is happiness has never danced in the rain.
—Unknown

Life may not be the party we hoped for, but while we're here we should dance.
—Unknown

Those who dance are considered insane
by those who cannot hear the music.
—Unknown

Remember, Ginger Rogers did everything Fred Astaire did,
but she did it backwards and in high heels.
—Faith Whittlesey

Daughters

Lessons Learned from My Daughter:
* Not all birds die when rescued and put in a box.
* Laundry can be done every two weeks if one has enough clothing
  and underwear.
* Books are to be read in the bathtub.
* Why do today what can be put off until midnight.
* Not all shy children stay that way.
* There is strength in being tall and beautiful.
* Food should be fast and tasty.
* Why drink water when one can slurp an icee.
* Small children and little sisters are extremely annoying.
* Large garden caterpillars are actually tomorrow's' butterflies.
* There's no such thing as having too many stuffed animals.
* Closets should be properly organized using plastic containers
  and color -coded hangers.
* Some children become athletic in high school.
* There is strength in being quiet and gentle.
* Anyone can be suspect in stealing a chicken.
* Only your little sister can be suspect when something is
  missing around the house.
* Respect can be earned without being loud and pushy.
* One can never read too many books.
* Bed sheets need never be changed; they always work the way they are.
* Vacuuming is optional as well.
* Forget cleaning sinks and toilets while we're at it.
* Spare time should be spent reading, not cleaning.
* Some children are admired by many people for helping and doing wonderful
things that you'll never know about.
* There's no such thing as overfeeding a chicken.
* One can never see too many movies.
* One can never have too many cats.
* One can never have too much clothing.
* One can love a chicken.

—Mary Roush
"Things I've learned from Serina"

Deservingness

Ask for what you want and be prepared to get it.
—Maya Angelou American poet, writer, and actress

If you want the best in your personal and professional life –
Never settle for less than you deserve.
—Debbie Allen, Speaker, Author "Confessions of Shameless Self Promoters"
www.DebbieAllen.com

Remember, you are always in the Divine flow of the Universe...
Even when you don't think you are.
It's really about remembering that you are the one who gets to choose
which universal stream you swim within.
"Row, row, row your boat gently down the stream, merrily, merrily, merrily,
merrily, life is but a dream."
Live the dreams that make you quiver with delight!
Ariel Fernandez, Aromatherapist & Educator
www.blissSville.com

I thank God I don't get what I deserve.
--Stephanie Moles, Founder of The Woman's Heart-Helping Women Come
Home, www.TheWoman'sHeart.org

The more you say no to what you don't want,
the more the Universe gives you what you do want.
—Peggy O'Neill, Speaker, Author "Walking Tall:Overcoming Inner Smallness
No Matter What Size You Are"
Small Miracles Unlimited, www.YoPeggy.com

You don't get what you deserve.
You get what you THINK you deserve.
—Oprah Winfrey

Destiny

Have you lived today with passion and purpose?
Have you loved unconditionally?
Have you hugged someone today?
Have you seized these 24 hours as if they were your last?
Have you celebrated life today?

We are made for larger ends than Earth can encompass.
Oh, let us be true to our exalted destiny.
—Catherine Booth

If you don't care where you're headed, any road will take you there.
—Wisdom of the Cheshire Cat from "Alice-in-Wonderland"

In every single decision we make, there is power—
the power to shape and control our own lives.
—Jo Condrill, Speaker, Author, "Take Charge of Your Life:
Dare to Pursue Your Dreams", www.goalminds.com

No trumpets sound when the important decisions of our life are made.
Destiny is made known silently.
—Agnes De Mille

Even when it's not what you want, it is!
—Terry Francis

We are commanded to love God with all our minds, as well as with all our
hearts, and we commit a great sin if we forbid or prevent that cultivation
of the mind in others which would enable them to perform this duty.
—Angelina Grimke

Our journey is to discover the questions that will enchant the answers
within us to come out dancing.
—Mary Marcdante, Speaker, Author "My Mother, My Friend: The Ten Most
Important Things to Talk About With Your Mother"
www.MaryMarcdante.com

You have arrived and you're in the driver's seat!
—Maria Marsala
www.ElevatingYou.com

In all of us is the capacity to shape our destiny.
—Mary Manin Morrissey

I knew what my job was; it was to go out and meet the people and love them.
—Diana, Princess of Wales

Do not follow where the path may lead.
Go instead where there is no path and leave a trail.
—Unknown

Your thoughts become your words.
Your words become your actions.
Your actions become your habits.
Your habits become your character.
Your character becomes your destiny.
-Unknown

I am an artist... I am here to live out loud.
—Emile Zola

Diversity & Equality

The Declaration of Independence of the 13 United States of America

We hold these truths to be self-evident,
that all men are created equal,
that they are endowed by their Creator with certain inalienable Rights,
that among these are Life, Liberty, and the pursuit of Happiness.
That to secure these rights, Governments are instituted among Men,
deriving their just powers from the consent of the governed.
That whenever any Form of Government becomes destructive of these ends,
it is the Right of the People to alter or to abolish it,
and to institute new Government,
laying its foundation on such principles
and organizing its powers in such form,
as them shall seem most likely to effect their Safety and Happiness.
—Declaration of Independence—

We are like diamonds, multifaceted, adding to the brilliance of the whole.
—Eln Albert, Speaker, Author

We've chosen the path to equality, don't let them turn us around.
—Geraldine Ferraro
(The first woman to be nominated as Vice President of the United States)

If we are to achieve a richer culture, rich in contrasting values,
we must recognize the whole gamut of human potentialities, and so weave a
less arbitrary social fabric, one in which each diverse gift will find a fitting place.
—Margaret Mead

Though the term "Latina" is relatively new, Latina "spirit" is timeless.
With passion, strength, hope, compassion, and a sense of justice, Latinas
have stirred up controversy, stood up against the majority, created artistic
beauty and died for their beliefs. These women--these unsung heroes--have
made countless contributions to our society--sometimes against all odds.
Whatever path we choose, it is obviously passion in our efforts that will make
the greatest difference.
—Sylvia Mendoza, Journalist & Author, "The Book of Latina Women:
150 Vidas (Lives) of Passion, Strength & Success

Won't it be wonderful when human beings exude the same enthusiasm for
differences among people as they do for differences in nature?
—Peggy O'Neill, Speaker, Author "Walking Tall:Overcoming Inner Smallness
No Matter What Size You Are"
· Small Miracles Unlimited, www.YoPeggy.com

Let us challenge one another to govern with passion, to govern with zeal
and to govern with a sense of righteousness – but always mindful that we must
govern with respect and reference for our difference.
—Dawn Clark Netsch

In order for others to show you respect, you need to show them respect them
first. It's the universal law of tithing – give first what it is you wish to receive.
—Sheryl Roush, Speaker, Author "Sparkle-Tudes!"
www.SparklePresentations.com

We hold these truths to be self-evident, that all men and women are created
equal.
—Elizabeth Cady Stanton
Declaration of Sentiments, First Women's Rights Convention
Seneca Falls, New York, July, 1848

God is, stop searching.
Life is a gift! Stop blaming.
Each event an expansion! Stop crying!
Each human being a blessing! Stop hating.
—Joni Wilson, Voice Expert, Author "Thunder Behind the Silence:
When a Woman Finds Her Voice"
www.JoniWilsonVoice.com

Do It Anyway

People are often unreasonable, illogical, and self-centered;

Forgive them anyway.

If you are kind, people may accuse you of selfish, ulterior motives;

Be kind anyway.

If you are successful you will win some false friends and true enemies;

Succeed anyway.

If you are honest and frank, people may cheat you;

Be honest and frank anyway.

What you spend years building, someone could destroy overnight;

Build anyway.

If you find serenity and happiness, they may be jealous;

Be happy anyway.

The good you do today, people will often forget tomorrow;

Do good anyway.

Give the world the best you have, and it may never be enough;

Give the world the best you've got anyway.

You see, in the final analysis, it is between you and God;

It was never between you and them anyway.

—Mother Teresa—

Dogs

Sign posted in a Veterinarian's waiting room:
"Be back in 5 minutes. Sit! Stay!"

A few weeks after my surgery, I went out to play catch with my golden retriever. When I bent over to pick up the ball, my prosthesis fell out. The dog snatched it, and I found myself chasing him down the road yelling "Hey, come back here with my breast!"
—Linda Ellerbee

If you want to be liked, get a dog.
The people you work with are not your friends.
—Deborah Norville

Pets have a way of knowing what's going on with you, how you are feeling. There is nothing like giving your pet a big hug and taking advantage of that unconditional love.
—Debra Pestrak, Speaker, Author, www.DebraPestrak.com

Ever consider what dogs must think of us?
I mean, here we come back from a grocery store with the most amazing haul — chicken, pork, half a cow. They must think we're the greatest hunters on earth!
—Anne Tyler

To a dog the whole world is a smell.
—Unknown

Some days you're the dog, and some days you're the hydrant.
—Unknown

Dreams & Goals

To say yes,to your dreams, you have to sweat and roll up your sleeves and plunge both hands into life up to the elbows.
—Jean Anouilh

To meet my goals, I couldn't let up when I was playing tennis.
—Tracy Austin, Professional Tennis Player

It takes a lot of courage to show your dreams to someone else.
—Erma Bombeck

A soul without a high aim is like a ship without a rudder.
—Eileen Caddy

You can plant a dream.
—Anne Campbell

It is necessary to try to surpass one's self always;
this occupation ought to last as long as life.
—Queen Christina

Your goal should be out of reach but not out of sight.
—Anita DeFrantz

A PLAN is WHAT you're going to do.
A SCHEDULE is WHEN you're going to do it
If you don't SCHEDULE your PLAN
it may NEVER get DONE.
—Rita Emmett, Speaker, Author, "The Procrastinator's Handbook"
www.RitaEmmett.com

The path to a goal is hardly ever a straight line.
—Cath Kachur, Speaker, Artist, www.HumanTuneUp.com

Whatever God's dream about man may be,
it seems certain it cannot come true unless man cooperates.
—Stella Terrill Mann

Do your dream now! You'll find that once you commit to yourself, the Universe
gives you unlimited support, and creates even more options for you.
YOU CAN DO IT!
—Catherine Ann Nary, aka 'CAN-DO' "

Visualize your dreams, hold them strongly in your mind, and never waver
from those visions, no matter who says they're impossible. By this method,
many "impossible" dreams have been fully accomplished.
—Kay Presto, Speaker, Author "Create the Magic in YOUR Life"
Contributor to "Chicken Soup for the NASCAR Soul"

The future belongs to those who believe in the beauty of their dreams.
—Eleanor Roosevelt

Dreams draw us forward, towards an even more fulfilling, joyful and abundant
life. Dreams build bridges between where we are now and where we can be in
the future whether that means tomorrow, six months from now or ten years
from now. Fueling our inner drive, they make our feet light, our tasks exciting
instead of burdensome and our hopes infinitely possible.
—Julie Jordan Scott, www.5passions.com

Run toward your dreams . . . .you just might catch some!
—Jennifer Rousseau Sedlock, www.JenniferSpeaks.com

Advance confidently in the direction of your dream and dare to BE the
heroine in your own story.
—Marilyn Sprague-Smith, M.Ed.
Co-Author, "The Princess Principle: Women Helping Women Discover
Their Royal Spirit", www.ThePrincessPrinciple.com

What if we're all meant to be what we secretly dream?
What would you ask if you knew you could have anything?
Like the mighty oak sleeps in the heart of a seed . . .
Are there miracles in you and me?
What would I do today . . . If I Were Brave?
—Jana Stanfield, Singer, Songwriter
From the song "If I Were Brave"
www.JanaStanfield.com

Reach high, for stars lie hidden in your soul. Dream deep, for every dream
precedes the goal.
—Pamela Vaull Starr

Always have some project underway... an ongoing project that goes over from
day to day and thus makes each day a small unit of time.
—Lillian Troll

Nothing is as real as a dream.
The world can change around you, but your dream will not.
Responsibilities need not erase it.
Duties need not obscure it.
Because the dream is within you, no one can take it away.
—Unknown

Living your dreams is the first, but not the final step in building real
and lasting self-esteem.
—Francine Ward, Speaker, Author "Esteemable Acts:
10 Actions for Building Real Self-Esteem"

If you want to accomplish the goals of your life,
you have to begin with the Spirit.
—Oprah Winfrey

Education & Learning

If you are planning for a year, sow rice; if you are planning for a decade,
plant trees; if you are planning for a lifetime, educate people.
—Chinese Proverb

The situations are not what do us in
Our attitude is what makes us spin
Worry never accomplishes anything in life
It causes us strife
If we only knew
The answers are within you
Look at yourself and you will see
You can have life any way you want it to be
–Lisa R. Delman, Author "Letters from the Heart"
www.HeartfeltMatters.com

We are the painters of our own self-portraits and who we become,
next week, next year, or five years from now, will be determined by our
attitudes, our actions, and what we learn.
—Mary-Ellen Drummond, Speaker, Author "A Woman's Way to Incredible
Success in Business: Inspirational Advice and Real-Life Lessons from 20
Prominent Businesswomen", www.medrummond.com

Learning is never a waste as long as you can remember what you learned.
—Terry Freeman-Sweeney

We live at the level of our language.
Whatever we can articulate we can imagine or explore.
All you have to do to educate a child is leave them alone and
teach them to read.
—Ellen Gilcrist

Education is a loan to be repaid with gift of self.
—Lady Bird Johnson

The best-educated human being is the one who understands most
about the life in which he is placed.
—Helen Keller

Be a life long learner. Constantly be looking for ways to make your life easier,
to grow, and to be the person you are capable of becoming.
—Debra Pestrak, Speaker, Author "Playing with the Big Boys"
www.DebraPestrak.com

Enlightenment must come little by little-otherwise it would overwhelm.
—Idries Shah

Label on a child's Superman costume:
Wearing of this garment does not enable you to fly
—Unknown

Education is not a form of entertainment,
but a means of empowering people to take control of their lives.
—Unknown

Learning to live what you're born with is the process, the involvement,
the making of a life.
—Diane Wakoski

Every child is intelligent in her/his own way.
We, as adults (teachers) need to find the switch to that light bulb.
—Bonnie Weisser

Books were my pass to personal freedom.
I learned to read at age three, and soon discovered there was a whole world
to conquer that went beyond our farm in Mississippi.
—Oprah Winfrey

Energy is equal to desire and purpose.
—Sheryl Adams

Our energy is like a garden, if it is tended to with respect and love it will
nourish our life. Learning to live with our energy is an art. Learning to pace
ourselves, remembering to love ourselves and share with discernment when
we have the energy is a state of honor. This is our practice.
—Linda Cammarata, RN, International musician, www.LifeCoaching.net

Love the way the Universe works!
Energy flows where attention goes and attracts synchronistic moments
that are waiting for your attention. Make it positive!
—Mary Marcdante, Speaker, Author "Living with Enthusiasm"
www.MaryMarcdante.com

Energy comes naturally from living your passion.
Tap into your core purpose and the energy is
endless, effervescent and electric.
"Passion" is to "pass-I-on," to pass who you are on to others.
—Sheryl Roush, Speaker, Author "Sparkle-Tudes!"

Issues of control can crush or strangle the natural energy that gives life to
invention, productivity, and prosperity.
—Leslie Yerkes, Contributor "Business: The Ultimate Resource"
Co-author "Beans: Four Principles for Running a Business
in Good Times or Bad"

Controlled deep breathing helps the body to transform the air we breathe
into energy. The stream of energized air produced by properly executed
and controlled deep breathing produces a current of inner energy which
radiates throughout the entire body and can be channeled to the body
areas that need it the most, on demand.
—Nancy Zi

10 Ways to Know if You Have "Estrogen Issues"

1. Everyone around you has an attitude problem.
2. You're adding chocolate chips to your cheese omelet.
3. The dryer has shrunk every last pair of your jeans.
4. Your husband is suddenly agreeing to everything you say.
5. You're using your cellular phone to dial up every bumper sticker that says: "How's my driving-call 1-800-"
6. Everyone's head looks like an invitation to batting-practice.
7. Everyone seems to have just landed here from "outer space."
8. You can't believe they don't make a tampon bigger than Super Plus.
9. You're sure that everyone is scheming to drive you crazy.
10. The ibuprofen bottle is empty and you bought it yesterday.

—Anonymous

I'M OUT OF ESTROGEN AND I HAVE A GUN
-Bumper Sticker

NEXT MOOD SWING: 6 MINUTES
—Bumper Sticker

Don't think of it as getting hot flashes.
Think of it as your inner child playing with matches.
—Unknown

Exercise

The only reason I would take up jogging is so I could hear heavy breathing again.
—Erma Bombeck

I AM in shape. Round is a shape.
—Bumper Sticker

My grandmother, she started walking five miles a day when she was sixty. She's ninety-seven today—we don't know where the hell she is.
—Ellen Degeneres

Our feet on this body of ours love to take us for a walk.
They love to go to interesting places. And while on the way here and there, what happens is fragmented parts of ourselves get restored into some sense of wholeness again. Oh the magic of one foot in front of the other.
—Cath Kachur, Speaker, Educator, Author, Artist
www.humantuneup.com

I've been doing leg lifts faithfully for about fifteen years, and the only thing that has gotten thinner is the carpet where I have been doing the leg lifts.
—Rita Rudner

I prefer Hostess fruit pies to pop-up toaster tarts because they don't require so much cooking.
—Carrie Snow

I never worry about diets. The only carrots that interest me are the number you get in a diamond.
—Mae West

Failure & Mistakes

Failure is impossible.
—Susan B. Anthony

When you make a mistake, don't look back at it long.
Take the reason of the thing into your mind, and then look forward.
Mistakes are lessons of wisdom. The past cannot be changed.
The future is yet in your power.
—Phyllis Bottome, Novelist and Lecturer

Every great mistake has a halfway moment,
a split second when it can be recalled and perhaps remedied.
—Pearl S. Buck

Have you lived long enough to know that many of the biggest lessons that
you've learned in life have come from making mistakes?
—Rita Emmett - Recovering Procrastinator
Author of "The Procrastinator's Handbook" and "The Procrastinating Child: A
Handbook for Adults to Help Children Stop Putting Things Off"
www.RitaEmmett.com

Mistakes are nothing more than unexpected results.
—Pat Farrell, Author "101 Ways to GET A LIFE"
www.Pat-Farrell.com

Just don't give up trying to do what you really want to do.
Where there is love and inspiration, I don't think you can go wrong.
—Ella Fitzgerald

Who has never tasted what is bitter does not know what is sweet.
—German Proverb

It's through adversity and failure that we ultimately win. Being able to see failure as an opportunity and improvement is critical to becoming unstoppable.
—Cynthia Kersey, Speaker, Author "Unstoppable" 45 powerful stories of perseverance and triumph
www.Unstoppable.net

Mistakes are part of the dues one pays for a full life.
—Sophia Loren

The most successful people in life fail forward fast. We all fail in life - it's how we learn and grow. The difference is successful people learn from their failures, it allows them to make better decisions in the future, and move forward quickly.
—Debra Pestrak, Speaker, Author "Playing with the Big Boys"
www.DebraPestrak.com

All human beings have failings, all human beings have needs and temptations and stresses. Men and women who live together through long years get to know one another's failings; but they also come to know what is worthy of respect and admiration in those they live with and in themselves. If at the end one can say, This man used to the limit the powers that God granted him; he was worthy of love and respect and of the sacrifices of many people, made in order that he might achieve what he deemed to be his task, then that life has been lived well and there are no regrets.
—Eleanor Roosevelt

On this day I will make more mistakes . . . and eat more ice cream.
—Nadine Stair

Experience is a wonderful thing. It enables us to recognize a mistake when we make it again.
—Unknown

Think like a queen. A queen is not afraid to fail.
Failure is another steppingstone to greatness.
—Oprah Winfrey

Faith

Be patient. God isn't finished with me yet.
—Bumper Sticker

I feel no need for any other faith than my faith in the kindness of human beings. I am so absorbed in the wonder of earth and the life upon it that I cannot think of heaven and angels.
—Pearl S. Buck

I see heaven's glories shine and faith shines equal . . .
—Emily Bronte

Lift your sights. Look at the stars, especially when things seem darkest. Know that there is a higher power in the universe. You are not alone.
—Jo Condrill, Speaker, Author, "Take Charge of Your Life:
Dare to Pursue Your Dreams", www.goalminds.com

Faith is the pierless bridge supporting what we see unto the scene that we do not.
—Emily Dickinson

It's the moment you think you can't that you realize you can.
—Celine Dion

God always delivers - with pepperoni.
—Linnda Durre', Ph.D., Dreams Come True Enterprises, LLC

Flowers find cracks in the concrete....And make it through.
Faith. Keep it.
—Cath Kachur, Speaker, Artist
ww.HumanTuneUp.com

A person consists of his faith. Whatever is his faith, even so is he.
—Indian Proverb

Faith is not making religious-sounding noises in the daytime.
It is asking your inmost self questions at night—and then getting up
and going to work.
—Mary Jean Iron

Weave in faith and God will find the thread.
—Proverb

Having faith in a Source greater than and one with myself has empowered
me to breakthrough every setback in my life — and I would not trade any of
those events for the character it's developed in me. God is always working
Her plan! Walk every day with faith!
—Sheryl Roush, Speaker, Author "Sparkle-Tudes!"
www.SparklePresentations.com

Faith is a curious thing.
It must be renewed; it has its own spring.
—Gladys Taber

Physical strength is measured by what we can carry;
spiritual by what we can bear.
—Unknown

Faith is like electricity.
You can't see it, but you can see the light.
—Unknown

Family

If you have only one smile in you, give it to the people you love.
Don't be surly at home, then go out in the street and start grinning
"Good morning" at total strangers.
—Maya Angelou

GOD MADE US SISTERS, PROZAC MADE US FRIENDS.
— Bumper Sticker

Your success as family, our success as a society, depends not on what
happens in the White House, but on what happens inside your house.
—Barbara Bush

If you don't have enough room for all your stuff, you don't need more room,
you need less stuff.
—Rita Emmett - Recovering Procrastinator
Author "The Procrastinator's Handbook" and "The Procrastinating Child:
A Handbook for Adults to Help Children Stop Putting Things Off"
www.RitaEmmett.com

The family unit plays a critical role in our society and in the training of the
generation to come.
—Sandra Day O'Connor

If you want the best seat in the house, you'll have to move the cat.
—Gail Rossi, Gallery Owner, Cat Alley   >^..^<
www.CatAlley.net

I've definitely never had to look very far outside my family for inspiration.
I'm surrounded by unbelievable strength and courage. Even in very difficult
times, there's always been a lot of humor and laughter.
—Maria Shriver, interviewed in *More* Magazine; May 2004

Fear

F - E - A - R
"False Evidence Appearing Real"

It doesn't matter how deep the water is, as long as you're floating.
—Penny Abshire, professional voice talent

If you knew Who walks beside you on the way that you have chosen,
fear would be impossible.
—A Course in Miracles

If you were to look up the word "renew" in the dictionary, it means,
"to make new again, to repair, to transform, to return to its original state."
In order for us to renew ourselves, change must accompany it.
Change can be radical, or in baby steps. Embrace it.
Change of any kind involves alternating, varying, and modifying old habits
with new revised healthy habits. A renewed transformation will awaken your
deep-rooted gems that are waiting to surface. Change will excavate a limitless
belief, and faith in yourself. It will unravel a newfound awareness of your
sparkling self. The fear of change will invariably raise its ugly head, and like
a lurking gremlin will terrorize, and sabotage our best intentions. Sound the
alarm, when you hear statements like 'you cannot do that' or 'it never worked
for you in the past'! Caress and hold the changes in your life close to you, and
free yourself from fear of change.
—Adele Alfano, Author "Expert Women Who Speak . . . Speak Out!
Life, Balance & Success Strategies by Women, for Women"

Fear is the gatekeeper of your comfort zone.
Your comfort zone is whatever is familiar to you.
Your comfort zone is what you are comfortable with, where you feel safe.
But how satisfying is safe? Fear keeps us from feeling alive when there's a
danger of not being accepted, approved, or understood.
Therefore we deny our essential nature.
—Rhonda Britten, Speaker, Author "Fearless Living:

✳ 79 ✳

Managing your fear is a temporary solution to a permanent problem, like putting a lid on a pressure cooker that's sure to blow sooner or later. Mastering your fear means accepting it, owning it, and making it work for you instead of against you.
—Rhonda Britten, Speaker, Author "Fearless Living: Live Without Excuses and Love Without Regret"

Nothing in life is to be feared. It is only to be understood.
—Madame Marie Curie

We need to learn to take our focus off fears, doubts, worries and insecurities, and place it instead upon faith and a belief that all will work out.
—Amy E. Dean

Ultimately we know deeply that the other side of every fear is a freedom.
—Marilyn Ferguson

Sixty seconds of preparation saves hours of trepidation.
—Anita Jefferson

When I dare to be powerful, to use my strength in the service of my vision, then it becomes less and less important whether I am afraid.
—Audre Lorde

What's holding you back from getting on with your life, is most often fear – fear of failure, fear of success, fear of rejection, fear of loss, fear of quitting, fear of you-name-it. Once you name the fear, it won't magically disappear, but it will lose some of its power over you and allow you to take another step forward.
—Mary Marcdante, Speaker, Author "Living with Enthusiasm: How the 21-Day Smile Diet Can Change Your Life"
www.MaryMarcdante.com

What stops us is fear. What frees us is courage.
—Debra Pestrak, Speaker, Author "Playing with the Big Boys"
www.DebraPestrak.com

Focus

You have to block everything out and be extremely focused and be relaxed and mellow too.
—Jennifer Capriati

All successful people are purpose and focus driven.
Awareness is really the partner of focus.
—Susan L. Gilbert, Author "The Land of I Can" and America's Focus Expert!

Patience is the ability to idle your motor
when you feel like stripping your gears.
—Barbara Johnson

If you surrender completely to the moments as they pass,
you live more richly those moments.
—Anne Morrow Lindbergh

We're all a lot more capable than we realize, but we lose our direction.
There comes a time when we need to tune out the world and listen to
our hearts.
—Thelma Mariano
www.u-unlimited.ca

What you focus on is what you get. If you focus on what you don't have,
what you don't think is possible, that is what will be in your life. If you focus
on the awesome person you are, that you can have anything you can dream,
then that's what is possible.
—Debra Pestrak, Speaker, Author "Playing with the Big Boys"
www.MostPowerfulWomen.com and www.DebraPestrak.com

Forgiveness

We are told that people stay in love because of chemistry,
or because they remain intrigued with each other,
because of many kindnesses, because of luck . . .
But part of it has got to be forgiveness and gratefulness.
—Ellen Goodman, US journalist

. . . forgive us our trespasses as we forgive those who trespass against us . . .
—The Lord's Prayer

We all want most to receive the love and peace of the Divine in our minds and
hearts. We are each a piece of God yearning for the peace of God. Forgiveness
brings us to a high resonance of that peace and that love.
Resolution is dealing with the parent inside our own heads, the internalized
thoughts, feelings, and messages; where is there resentment?
Reconciliation means that we are 100% responsible for the interactions in our
relationships and the results therein.
Receiving God's love moves us from pain to pilgrimage, from adversity into
adventure, from travail into a trail, and from problems into possibilities.
—Mary Manin Morrissey

Learn to forgive yourself first. It makes it easier to forgive others.
—Debra Pestrak, Speaker, Author "Playing with the Big Boys"
www.DebraPestrak.com

Carrying a resentment is like taking poison
and waiting for the other person to die.
—Unknown

The practice of forgiveness is our most important contribution
to the healing of the world.
—Marianne Williamson

Freedom

I've never understood why people consider youth a time of freedom and joy.
It's probably because they have forgotten their own.
Margaret Atwood, Novelist and Poet

I used to think freedom meant doing whatever you want.
Now, it means knowing who you are, what you are supposed to be doing
on this earth, and then simply doing it.
—Natalie Goldberg

Dear God,
Do you draw the lines around the countries?
If you don't, who does?
—Nan
Kid's Theology

Freedom is knowing who you really are.
—Linda Thomson

The key to inspiration is accountability.
Inspiration is the freedom and the joy we find
on the other side of being responsible,
even when we don't want to be.
When we are that, we inspire even ourselves.
—Pamela Truax
www.AccountabilityPays.com

Friendship

A friend is known when needed.
—Arabian Proverb

There is nothing I would not do for those who are really my friends. I have no notion of loving people by halves.
—Jane Austin, 1775 -1817, British writer

Time is money, but friends are priceless.
—Marie Betts-Johnson, speaker, international etiquette goddess

A friend is someone you can be alone with and have nothing to do
and not be able to think of anything to say and be comfortable in the silence.
—Sheryl Condie

Thank You Friend,
I never came to you, my friend, and went away without some new enrichment of the heart; More faith and less of doubt, more courage in the days ahead.
And often in great need coming to you, I went away comforted indeed.
How can I find the shining word, the glowing phrase that tells all that your love has meant to me, all that your friendship spells? There is no word, no phrase for you on whom I so depend. All I can say to you is this, God bless you precious friend.
—Grace Noll Crowell

No one is rich enough to do without a neighbor.
—Danish Proverb

It is the friends you can call up at 4AM that matter.
—Marlene Dietrich

One who looks for a friend without faults will have none.
—Hasidic Saying

Who finds a faithful friend, finds a treasure.
—Jewish Saying

Plant a seed of friendship; reap a bouquet of happiness.
—Lois L. Kaufman

Laugh and the world laughs with you. Cry and you cry with your girlfriends.
—Laurie Kuslansky

Your friendship is a glowing ember Through the year;
and each December From its warm and living spark
We kindle flame against the dark
And with its shining radiance light
Our tree of faith on Christmas night.
—Thelma J. Lund

I always thought that the great high privilege, relief and comfort of friendship
was that one had to explain nothing.
—Katherine Mansfield

Hold a true friend with both your hands.
—Nigerian Proverb

In a friend you find a second self.
—Isabelle Norton

If you have true friends, treasure them, as they are pure gold.
—Kay Presto, Speaker, Author "Create the Magic in YOUR Life"
Contributor to "Chicken Soup for the NASCAR Soul"

A friend is someone who doesn't like the same people you do.
—Proverb

The time to make friends is before you need them.
—Proverb

A friend hears the song in my heart and sings it to me when my memory fails.
—*Readers Digest*

It is not what you give your friend, but what you are willing to give her
that determines the quality of friendship.
—Mary Dixon Thayer

Only your real friends will tell you when your face is dirty.
—Sicilian Proverb

The best antiques are old friends.
—Unknown

The miracle of friendship can be spoken without words . . .
hearing unspoken needs, recognizing secret dreams,
understanding the silent things that only true friends know.
—Unknown

To each one of us friendship has a different meaning. For all of us it is a gift.
Friendship needs to be cherished and nurtured. It needs to be cultivated on a
daily basis. Then shall it germinate and yield its fruit.
—Unknown

Everyone hears what you say, friends listen to what you say,
but best friends listen to what you don't say.
—Unknown

A good friend is someone who can drive you nuts, but will be the first person
you call when you win that all expenses paid dream vacation.
—Michelle Weisser

Fun & Playfulness

When the heart opens, the soul comes out to play.
In this exalted state, life expands, from the inside out.
—Perry A, Author "People Are Just Desserts"
www.PerryA.com

Life loves to be taken by the lapel and told, "I am with you kid—Let's go!"
—Maya Angelou, American poet, writer, and actress

Seize the moment.
Remember all those women on the Titanic who waved off the dessert cart.
—Erma Bombeck, American Humorist

Adventure is worthwhile.
—Amelia Earhart

As long as I can focus on enjoying what I'm doing, having fun,
I know I'll play well.
—Steffi Graf, Professional Tennis Player

To love what you do and feel that it matters — how could anything be more fun?
—Katherine Graham

If you always do what interests you, at least one person is pleased.
—Katharine Hepburn

If you obey all the rules, you miss all the fun.
— Katharine Hepburn

Fly a kite or play Frisbee.
Juggle badly.
Go to a playground - use the climbing equipment and swings.
Howl at the moon!
—Thelma Mariano

The more things you love doing, the more enthusiasm you'll feel about your life,
your work, and your sense of who you are.
As you go about your day, ask other people,
"What did you love doing as a child?"
"What games or activities did you play?"
"What do you love doing in your life now?"
"What would you love to do in the future?"
—Mary Marcdante, Speaker, Author "Living with Enthusiasm:
How the 21-Day Smile Diet Can Change Your Life"
www.MaryMarcdante.com

You are Yippee and Yummy and Yeasty and Youthful.
You are Exuberant and Effervescent and Eloquent and Eternal.
You are Spirited and Sensual and Sensational and Silly.
Choose one of the above and BE that all day, thus creating YES! moments daily.
—Dianne Onstad, Co-author of "ABC's of YES! ~ Actions For Success"
www.MagicOfYes.com

Treat life like a rental car. Take chances and have lots of fun with it!
—Unknown

The Master in the art of living makes little distinction between his work
and his play, his labor and his leisure, his mind and his body, his education
and his recreation, his love and his religion. He hardly knows which is which.
He simply pursues his vision of excellence in whatever he does, leaving others
to decide whether he is working or playing. To him he is always doing both.
—Zen Buddhist Text

Funny Signs

On a Septic Tank Truck sign:
"We're #1 in the #2 business."

* * *

Sign over a Gynecologist's Office:
"Dr. Jones, at your cervix."

* * *

On a Plumber's truck:
"We repair what your husband fixed."

* * *

On a Plumber's truck:
"Don't sleep with a drip. Call your plumber."

* * *

Pizza Shop Slogan:
"7 days without pizza makes one weak."

* * *

At a Tire Shop in Milwaukee:
"Invite us to your next blowout."

* * *

On a Plastic Surgeon's Office door:
"Hello. Can we pick your nose?"

* * *

At a Towing company:
"We don't charge an arm and a leg. We want tows."

* * *

Spotted in a toilet of an office:
"TOILET OUT OF ORDER.
PLEASE USE FLOOR BELOW."

On an Electrician's truck:
"Let us remove your shorts."

* * *

On a Maternity Room door:
"Push. Push. Push."

* * *

At an Optometrist's Office
"If you don't see what you're looking for,
you've come to the right place."

* * *

In a Podiatrist's office:
"Time wounds all heels."

* * *

Outside a Muffler Shop:
"No appointment necessary.
We hear you coming."

* * *

At the Electric Company:
"We would be delighted if you send in your payment.
However, if you don't, you will be."

* * *

In the front yard of a Funeral Home:
"Drive carefully. We'll wait."

* * *

Seen in a department store:
"BARGAIN BASEMENT UPSTAIRS"

* * *

Notice in a open field:
"The farmer allows walkers to cross the field for free,
But the Bull charges."

ETERNITY:
Smoking or Nonsmoking?

Future

Never be afraid to trust an unknown future to a known God.
—Corrie Ten Boom

If you want to know your past, look into your present conditions.
If you want to know your future, look into your present actions.
—Buddhist Saying

We cannot let the past cloud our perception of the future.
—Karen Chikodroff

The future will take care of itself. I am in charge of taking care of the present.
--Stephanie Moles, www.TheWoman'sHeart.org

The future belongs to those who believe in the beauty of their dreams.
—Eleanor Roosevelt

The past cannot be changed. The future is yet in your power.
—Mary Pickford

The future lies before you, like paths of pure white snow.
Be careful how you tread it, for every step will show.
—Unknown

Wanna make God laugh? Plan your future.
—Unknown

Always remember the future comes one day at a time.
—Unknown

I find it interesting that the meanest life, the poorest existence, is attributed to God's will, but as human beings become more affluent, as their living standard and style begin to ascend the material scale, God descends the scale of responsibility at a commensurate speed.
—Maya Angelou, American poet, writer, and actress

Seeking God is more than having a casual interest in Him.
It's similar to going on a hunt, and the place for us to start is God's Word, where He reveals Himself to us.
—Ellen Banks Elwell

I recommend running away sometimes.
—God
(submitted by Cath Kachur)

Dear God,
How did you know you were God?
Who told you?
—Charlene
"Kid's Theology"

When the heart and mind are truly open, I can remember to hear with God's ears, speak with His tongue, and see with His eyes. My ears will not hear through my fear, I will not speak from my fear, nor will I see you in the light of my fear. It will be with love.
--Stephanie Moles, www.TheWoman'sHeart.org

Quiet your spirit, submit your intellect, and you will hear OUR GOD'S spirit.
—Mona M. Mordoff, Speaker,
Ministry-KWJWD - Know What Jesus Would Do

Be willing to believe in a greater way about yourself.
Let your heart be receptive to God's Spirit and guidance.
Have the courage to make the decision to allow the possibility of greatness
 in you. Take risks beyond your boundaries, and God is right there with you.
—Mary Manin Morrissey, Author "Life Keys"

The biggest risk I ever took was not listening to God,
figuring I could do it on my own and not clearing it with him first.
You can imagine what the consequences were.
—Della Reese, Actress, Minister, TV Series "Touched By An Angel"

What you are is God's gift to you.
What you become is your gift to God.
—Eleanor Roosevelt

God can only do FOR you what He can do THROUGH you.
—Sheryl Roush, Speaker, Author "Sparkle-Tudes!"
www.SparklePresentations.com

If we open our hearts to God, He has promised to work within us.
—Margaret Thatcher

Without His love I can do nothing, with His love there is nothing I cannot do.
—Unknown

God does not ask about our ability, but our availability.
—Unknown

If you believe in an unseen Christ, you will believe in the unseen
Christ-like potential of others.
—Unknown

God is definitely out of the closet.
—Marianne Williamson, Speaker, Author

Gratitude

H - heal your heart
E - exercise your emotions
A - accept your uniqueness
R - relax and trust
T – thankfulness

—Adele Alfano, author "Expert Women Who Speak . . . Speak Out!, "
and "Life, Balance & Success Strategies by Women, for Women "

Gratitude unlocks the fullness of life. It turns what we have into enough,
and more. It turns denial into acceptance, chaos to order, confusion to clarity.
It can turn a meal into a feast, a house into a home, a stranger into a friend.
Gratitude makes sense of our past, brings peace for today, and creates a vision
for tomorrow.
—Melody Beattie, Author "Codependent No More," and
"Beyond Codependency"

Because gratification of a desire leads to the temporary stilling of the mind
and the experience of the peaceful, joyful Self it's no wonder that we get
hooked on thinking that happiness comes from the satisfaction of desires.
This is the meaning of the old adage, "Joy is not in things, it is in us."
—Joan Borysenko

Both abundance and lack exist simultaneously in our lives, as parallel realities.
It is always our conscious choice which secret garden we will tend . . . when we
choose not to focus on what is missing from our lives but are grateful for the
abundance that's present — love, health, family, friends, work, the joys of nature
and personal pursuits that bring us pleasure — the wasteland of illusion falls
away and we experience Heaven on earth.
—Sarah Ban Breathnach, Author "Simple Abundance"

Never hesitate to celebrate, commiserate, or commemorate before it is too late.
—Cynthia Brian, speaker, radio and TV show host
Author "Chicken Soup for the Gardener's Soul"
www.bethestaryouare.org

Gratitudes are actions you can take that refine your ability to distinguish between the world of fear and the world of freedom, between fear-based feelings and your freedom-based intuition. When you consciously choose to see the good that is already present in your life, you immediately open up the floodgates for more good to come your way.
—Rhonda Britten, Speaker, Author "Fearless Living: Live Without Excuses and Love Without Regret"

Gratitude is the heart's memory.
—French Proverb

Normal day let me be aware of the treasure you are.
—Mary Jean Iron

One can never pay in gratitude; one can only pay "in kind" somewhere else in life.
—Anne Morrow Lindbergh

Creating more success in your life is not about what you deserve or have to earn; it's about what and how much you appreciate. Sincere appreciation is one of the best investments you can make in your life. Appreciation pays!
—Mary Marcdante , Author of "Living with Enthusiasm"
www.MaryMarcdante.com

Walk the world with gratitude.
—St. John's United Church of Christ, 1957 Sermon

Gratitude is our most direct line to God and the angels.
If we take the time, no matter how crazy and troubled we feel, we can find something to be thankful for. The more we seek gratitude, the more reason the angels will give us for gratitude and joy to exist in our lives.
—Terry Lynn Taylor

The more you praise and celebrate your life,
 the more there is in life to celebrate.
—Oprah Winfrey

Guidance

When I meditated on the word GUIDANCE, I kept seeing "dance" at the end of the word. I remember reading that doing God's will is a lot like dancing. When two people try to lead, nothing feels right. The movement doesn't flow with the music, and everything is quite uncomfortable and jerky.

When one person realizes and lets the other lead, both bodies begin to flow with the music. One gives gentle cues, perhaps with a nudge to the back or by pressing lightly in one direction or another. It's as if two become one body, moving beautifully. The dance takes surrender, willingness, and attentiveness from one person and gentle guidance and skill from the other.

My eyes drew back to the word GUIDANCE.
When I saw "G," I thought of God, followed by "u" and "i."
"God, "u" and "i" dance."! God, you, and I dance.
This statement is what guidance means to me.

As I lowered my head, I became willing to trust that I would get guidance about my life. Once again, I became willing to let God lead.

I Hope You Dance !!!!!!!!!!!!

—Julia Jensen

Happiness

Happiness is a conscious choice, not an automatic response.
— Mildred Barthel

Happiness is good health and a bad memory.
—Ingrid Bergman

Celebrate the happiness that friends are always giving,
make every day a holiday and celebrate just living!
—Amanda Bradley, Poet, Author

Let the sun shine in your gardens and the stars in your heart.
—Cynthia Brian, speaker, radio and TV show host
Author of "Chicken Soup for the Gardener's Soul"
www.star-style.com www.bethestaryouare.org

Many persons have a wrong idea of what constitutes happiness.
It is not attained through self-gratification, but through fidelity to a
worthy purpose.
—Helen Keller

I'm fulfilled in what I do . . . I never thought that a lot of money or fine clothes —
the finer things of life — would make you happy. My concept of happiness
is to be filled in a spiritual sense.
—Coretta Scott King

Happiness for the average person may be said to flow largely from
common sense — adapting one-self to circumstances — and a sense of humor.
—Beatrice Lillie, English comedienne

What a man really wants is creative challenge with sufficient skills
to bring him within the reach of success so that he may have the
expanding joy of achievement.
—Fay B. Nash

If my heart can become pure and simple like that of a child,
I think there probably can be no greater happiness than this.
—Kitaro Nishida

I experience my greatest joy when looking into the loving eyes and joyful smiles
on the faces of elderly. It is in those special moments that I truly believe in God's
grace and the magnitude with which one person can make an incredible
difference. I truly believe that it is in giving to another that we find our greatest
gift—the gift of giving of oneself. Your touch, holding the hand of another, giving
a hug, or being face-to-face with the humanity is where you will find your most
accomplished and challenging space to serve. Go for it! Your happiness is a
decision of your heart.
—Candace Pittenger, Speaker, Aging Expert
Author, "Happiness is a Decision of the Heart"
www.agetalk.com, www.GenAmericaServe.com

Happiness is a sunbeam which may pass through a thousand bosoms without
losing a particle of its original ray; nay, when it strikes on a kindred heart, like
the converged light on a mirror, it reflects itself with redoubled brightness.
It is not perfected till it is shared.
—Jane Porter

Our happiness in this world depends on the affections we are able to inspire.
—Duchess Prazlin

All the days of the oppressed are wretched,
but the cheerful heart has a continual feast.
—Proverbs 15:15

A merry heart does good like medicine.
—Proverbs 17:22

It is not easy to find happiness in ourselves,
and it is not possible to find it elsewhere.
—Agnes Repplier

Happiness is not a state to arrive at, but a manner of traveling.
—Margaret Lee Runbeck

A happy woman is one who has no cares at all; a cheerful woman is one who
has cares but doesn't let them get her down.
—Beverly Sills

Happiness walks on busy feet.
—Kitte Turmell

The surest way to happiness is to lose yourself
in a cause greater than yourself.
—Unknown

Cheerfulness is contagious, but don't wait to catch it from others.
Be a carrier.
—Unknown

Who ever said money can't bring happiness
didn't know where to shop.
—Unknown

Being happy doesn't mean everything is perfect.
It means you have decided to look beyond the imperfections.
—Unknown

Joy, has no cost.
—Marianne Williamson, Author "A Woman's Worth"

Have a Sense of Humor

Humor comes from self-confidence.
—Rita Mae Brown

Comedy is tragedy plus time.
—Carol Burnett

The one important thing I've learned over the years is the difference
between taking one's work seriously and one's self seriously.
The first is imperative; the second is disastrous.
—Dame Margot Fonteyn

WARNING: Humor may be hazardous to your illness.
—Ellie Katz

"Federal Expresso"
When you absolutely, positively, have to stay up all night.
—Diane Reamy

A sense of humor is the lubricant of life's machinery.
—Unknown

If you can look into the mirror without laughter,
you have no sense of humor.
—Unknown

That is the best — to laugh with someone
because you both think the same things are funny.
— Gloria Vanderbilt

Health

In one day:
Your heart will likely beat over 100,000 times
Your blood will travel about 168,000 miles
You will breathe about 23,000 times
You will eat over three pounds of food
You will drink three pounds of liquids
You will turn in your sleep 25-30 times
You may speak about 48,000 words
You will use some 7,000,000 brain cells

Never go to a doctor whose office plants have died.
—Erma Bombeck

Pampering is preventative medicine, not a recuperative strategy after crashing.
—Beth Burns, Professional Life Coach, www.BrightSideCoaching.com

Seasonal foods nourish us.. through tradition and warm remembrances, and
fortify our bodies. Cooking with foods of the season allows us to enjoy foods
when they are most flavorful, the brightest in color, and most abundant in juice
and texture—when they are perfect gifts from nature. They need little
adornment or fatty sauces.
—Lesa Heebner, Speaker, Author "Cooking with the Seasons"

Dear Mr. God,
I wish you would not make it so easy for people to come apart.
I had to have 3 stitches and a shot.
—Janet
Kid's Theology

Who ever thought up the word "Mammogram?"
Every time I hear it, I think I'm supposed to put my breast in an envelope
and send it to someone.
—Jan King

The more enthusiasm you have, the healthier you feel and the faster you heal, whether you're recovering from an illness, accident, broken heart, death of a loved one, end of a marriage, or any other type of loss. Research has now proven that laughter, optimism, and a will to live – all aspects of enthusiasm – speed up healing time and increase well-being and longevity.
—Mary Marcdante, Speaker, Author
www.MaryMarcdante.com

I am radiantly beautiful, vibrantly healthy, extraordinarily creative, abundantly wealthy, and full of boundless energy, joy and awe!
—Dianne Onstad, Co-author of "ABC's of YES! ~ Actions For Prosperity"
www.MagicOfYes.com

Never eat more than you can lift.
—Miss Piggy, From The Muppets

Chronic diseases on the rise like high blood pressure, Type 2 diabetes (high blood sugar) and high cholesterol all respond favorably to positive lifestyle change such as the addition of regular exercise and the consumption of more fruits and vegetables daily. We have the power to motivate ourselves toward positive change every day.
Thus the quote, "If something changes, then something changes."
—Mary Roush, RN, CDE, Patient Educator of Kauai Medical Clinic

A male gynecologist is like an auto mechanic who never owned a car.
—Carrie Snow

Always take a good look at what you're about to eat. It's not so important to know what it is, but it's critical to know what it was.
—Unknown

Heart disease continues to be the #1 cause of death in the U.S. I believe this is because we are a society of broken hearts. Practicing kindness and compassion toward ourselves and one another is one of the best antidotes for heart disease.
—Diana Weiss-Wisdom, Ph.D., Author "Stress and A Healthy Ticker: A Psychological Approach to Preventing Heart Disease"

Heart

There is nothing enduring in life for a woman except
what she builds in a man's heart.
—Judith Anderson

When people go to work, they shouldn't have to leave their hearts at home.
—Betty Bender

When your heart speaks, take good notes.
—Judith Campbell

I wear my heart on my sleeve.
—Diana, Princess of Wales

Within your heart, keep one still, secret spot where dreams may go.
—Louise Driscoll

The woman's vision is deep reaching, the man's far reaching.
With the man the world is his heart, with the woman the heart is her world.
—Betty Grable

What we have most to fear is failure of the heart.
—Sonia Johnson

More tears are shed over answered prayers than unanswered ones.
—Mother Teresa

Follow your heart, but be quiet for a while first.
Ask questions, then feel the answer. Learn to trust your heart.
—Unknown

Hobbies

If at first you don't succeed, then skydiving is not for you.
—Bumper Sticker

I've moved cities 6 times, countries and continents 3 times and always it has been the creation of a garden that has settled and calmed. Whether it is the gift of growing, the creation of something new, or the claiming of a space, I am not sure. But for me, gardening has been an essential part of re-establishment and of finding myself.
—Anne Frodsham, horticulturist

A hobby a day keeps the doldrums away.
—Phyllis McGinley

A hobby is hard work you wouldn't do for a living.
—Unknown

Passion Hobbies

Passion Hobbies are pastimes that have significant value,
something that we do to nurture our spirit and balance our balance.
These are activities that brings us joy, enlighten and center, enrich and
empower us. For most of us — it's what we do AFTER work that helps us
keep our sanity AT work.

Women in my seminars tell me their favorite passion hobbies include:
reading mystery or romance novels;
walking, running, aerobics or exercise;
making needlepoint and crafts for others;
jigsaw and crossword puzzles;
doing fun and playful things with their kids;
and of course, shopping makes this list every time!

I enjoy gathering my women friends for an evening out DANCING!
It's great exercise, safe and outrageous fun.

All the years growing up, I remember my father would rush home from work
and head out to the back yard where he would enjoy his passion hobby —
organic gardening. He would take out any of his frustrations, find his inner
peace, and then come into the house. I know for him (and for us) it allows time
to re-center and re-group from the day, helping him to lead a more balanced
life. Today, years after his retirement, it's STILL his passion hobby. A pastime
that has nurtured his spirit over the years, and brings a smile every time he
shares fresh fruits and vegetables with neighbors, friends and family.

My mother, on the other hand, loves to volunteer time to philanthropic groups
and organizations such as the U.S. Olympic Training Center — and received
Volunteer of the Year for her time and energy leading tour groups and helping
Olympians pack their gear for the upcoming events.

What passion hobbies do you currently have in your life —
or could to incorporate into your life on a regular basis that will
bring you pleasure, spiritual rejuvenation and greater life balance?

—Sheryl Roush, Speaker, Author "Sparkle-Tudes"
Contributing author to "The Princess Principle:
Women Helping Women Discover Their Royal Spirit"

Honesty & Integrity

Living with integrity means:

· Not settling for less than what you know
 you deserve in your relationships.

· Asking for what you want and need from others.

· Speaking your truth, even though it might
 create conflict or tension.

· Behaving in ways that are in harmony
 with your personal values.

· Making choices based on what you believe,
 and not what others believe.

—Barbara De Angelis

Strive always to keep conscience clear before God and man.
—Acts 24:16
Women's Devotional Bible 2, New International Version

In everything set them an example by doing what is good.
In your teaching show integrity, seriousness and soundness of speech that
cannot be condemned, so that those who oppose you may be ashamed
because they have nothing bad to say about us.
—Titus 2:7-8
Women's Devotional Bible 2, New International Version

If the writing is honest it cannot be separated from the one who wrote it.
—Unknown

Hope

While there's life, there's hope!
—Ancient Roman Saying

Expect to have hope rekindled.
Expect your prayers to be answered in wondrous ways.
The dry seasons in life do not last.
The spring rains will come again
—Sarah Ban Breathnach, Author "Simple Abundance"

Hope is the thing with feathers That perches in the soul
And sings the tune without the words And never stops at all.
—Emily Dickenson

Hope is the feeling you have that the feeling you have isn't permanent.
—Jean Kerr

The very least you can do in your life is to figure out what you hope for.
And the most you can do is live inside that hope. Not admire it from a
distance but live right in it, under its roof.
—Barbara Kingsolver

Hope is an action word. If I truly have hope then I need to act like it.
I will act like 'it' will work out, that life will make sense, that I will get to love
again, and that I will be grateful that I am alive - and that is enough.
--Stephanie Moles, www.TheWoman'sHeart.org

Hope sees the invisible, feels the intangible and achieves the impossible.
—Unknown

Hope has been and always will be safe. It's inside every one of us.
—Xena, Warrior Princess, TV Series

Human Spirit

You may encounter many defeats, but you must not be defeated.
In fact, it may be necessary to encounter the defeats,
so you can know who you are, what you can rise from,
how you can still come out of it.
—Maya Angelou, American poet, writer, and actress

You know God is within when all you see and do is done with love.
—Lydia Boyd, Past International Director, Toastmasters International

Climb every obstacle. Eliminate your limits.
—Anita Jefferson

The greatest natural resource in the world is not in the earth's waters or
minerals, nor in the forests or grasslands. It is the spirit that resides in every
unstoppable person. And the spirit of the individual benefits us all.
—Cynthia Kersey, Speaker, Author "Unstoppable" www.unstoppable.net

Take care of yourself . . . You are loved more than you will ever know!
—Sue Podany, Speaker, Author "Life In The Fast Lane . . . Balancing Tips
for the Stressed Out Professional!"
www.SuePodany.com

All endeavor calls for the ability to tramp the last mile, shape the last plan,
endure the last hours toil. The fight to the finish spirit is the one characteristic
we must possess if we are to face the future as finishers.
— Unknown

The beauty of the human thought process is that it is ever expanding.
It's always looking for new ways to solve old problems.
—Joni Wilson, Voice Expert, Author "The 3-Dimensional Voice"
www.JoniWilsonVoice.com

Ideas & Innovation

It's easier to edit than create.
—Cynthia Berger

Innovation:
Implementing new ideas that customers and users
value enough to actively support.
—Lynda Curtin, The Opportunity Thinker

If you throw enough mud on the wall, something is sure to stick!
—Irene Levitt, Author of "Brainwriting"
www.IreneLevitt.com

Ideas are God's currency.
—Mary Manin Morrissey, Author "Life Keys"

Ideas and their potential are at the center of the Universe.
The more ideas you have, acknowledge and share, the more abundant you
attract. If we do not take action on one of the Divine ideas we are gifted,
it returns to the big melting pot of consciousness for someone else to
scoop out.
—Sheryl Roush, Speaker, Author "Sparkle-Tudes!"
www.SparklePresentations.com

Las cosas claras y el chocolate espeso.
(Ideas should be clear and chocolate thick.)
—Spanish Proverb

The only people in the world who can change things
are those who can sell ideas.
—Lois Wyse

Inspirations

If there is light in the soul, there will be beauty in the person.
If there is beauty in the person, there will be harmony in the house.
If there is harmony is the house, there will be order in the nation.
If there is order in the nation, there will be peace in the world.
—Chinese Proverb

Life is like a Bubble.
You choose where you want to float and for how long.
—T. J. Barnes, RN, Business Life Coach

People are like stained-glass windows.
They sparkle and shine when the sun is out, but when the darkness sets in,
their true beauty is revealed only if there is a light from within.
—Elizabeth Kübler-Ross

How do you stay inspired?
Clear and simple: Who do you appreciate? Tell them!
What are you grateful for? Tell yourself.
What are you excited about? Tell the world!
—Mary Marcdante, Author of "Living with Enthusiasm," and
"My Mother, My Friend: The Ten Most Important Things to Talk About
With Your Mother"
www.MaryMarcdante.com

I know God will not give me anything I can't handle.
I just wish he didn't trust me so much.
—Mother Teresa

Intuition

Trust your hunches. They're usually based on facts filed away just below the conscious level.
—Dr. Joyce Brothers, Psychologist and Television Personality

Instinct is the nose of the mind.
—Madame de Girardin

Hunch. Gut feeling. Voice of God. Instinct. Many names. One Force.
—Cath Kachur, Speaker, Artist
ww.HumanTuneUp.com

Listen to your gutometer; it is always right.
—Jayne Murad, Director of Human Resources, Westin Los Angeles Airport

Women don't listen to the voice inside them.
We get our lives so busy—it [intuition] is a gift from God.
—Marie Osmond, on Oprah

Listen to your intuition, for it is your best friend,
Ignore your fears, for they are your enemy,
Believe in your dreams, for they are your future.
—Barbara Sanfilippo, Speaker, Author, "Dream Big! What's the Best
That Can Happen"
www.Barbara-Sanfilippo.com

The quiet voice inside says, "That's the way it should be…"
—Oprah Winfrey

Joy & Enthusiasm

Joy is the holy fire that keeps our purpose warm and our intelligence aglow.
—Helen Keller

Birds sing after a storm; why shouldn't people feel as free to delight in whatever sunlight remains to them?
—Rose Kennedy

Enthusiasm isn't about how old you are or how tall you are or what you do for a living. It's not about how loud you are, how much money you have, or what kind of car you drive. Enthusiasm is about how willing you are to be your biggest, brightest self in the world. It's about sharing with the world what makes you laugh, what delights you, what you're passionate about, and whom you love. And more importantly, sharing that love with yourself.
—Mary Marcdante, Speaker, Author "Living with Enthusiasm: How the 21-Day Smile Diet Can Change Your Life"
www.MaryMarcdante.com

Make your day by becoming and being the person who makes your heart smile.
—Maria Marsala
www.ElevatingYou.com

By vibing infectious joy, you can uplift sunken spirits, turn a smile, inspire hope, make someone's day, and maybe even change someone's life. So, next time you feel like jumping up and clicking your heels together, don't hold back. Do it!
—Peggy O'Neill, Speaker, Author "Walking Tall:Overcoming Inner Smallness No Matter What Size You Are"
Small Miracles Unlimited, www.YoPeggy.com

Reflect upon your blessings, for they are many and varied.
As the seasons revolve and change, so do the gifts that are presented.
Open to all the joy life wishes to give you.
—Dianne Onstad, Co-author of "ABC's of YES! ~ Actions For Success"
www.MagicOfYes.com

Life without Joy and Humor is like a car without an engine . . .
you can sit in it but you won't go very far!
—Sue Podany, speaker, author "Energy . . . 120 Easy Ways to Get It, Keep It,
and . . . Keep From Giving It Away!"
www.SuePodany.com

The light in the eyes of him whose heart is joyful,
rejoices the heart of others.
—Proverbs 15:30

A cheerful look brings joy to the heart,
and good news gives health to the bones.
—Proverbs 15:30
Women's Devotional Bible 2, New International Version

Joy is a net of love by which you can catch souls.
—Mother Teresa

Is Your Life an Expression of Your Pure Joy?
Do you live each day with Passion?
Is your life what you dreamed it could be?
No? Are you improving, but slowly?
Where are you on the Passion Scale?
Let's start. Right here, right now,
Living Passionately, Everyday!
—Julie Jordan Scott
www.5passions.com

Joy is what happens to us when we allow ourselves
to recognize how good things really are.
—Marianne Williamson

Kindness

The kindness and affection from the public have carried me through some of the most difficult periods, and always your love and affection have eased the journey.
—Diana, Princess of Wales

Whatever you give will find countless ways back to you.
—Dove Promises Chocolate inscription

As perfume to the flower, so is kindness to speech.
—Katherine Francke

The fruit of the Spirit is love, joy, peace, patience, kindness, goodness, faithfulness.
—Galatians 5:22
Women's Devotional Bible 2, New International Version

We are told that people stay in love because of chemistry,
or because they remain intrigued with each other,
because of many kindnesses, because of luck . . .
But part of it has got to be forgiveness and gratefulness.
—Ellen Goodman, US journalist

I have never met a person whose greatest need was anything other than real, unconditional love. You can find it in a simple act of kindness toward someone who needs help. There is no mistaking love. You feel it in your heart. It is the common fiber of life, the flame that heals our soul, energizes our spirit and supplies passion to our lives. It is our connection to God and to each other.
—Elizabeth Kubler-Ross

Politeness costs nothing and gains everything.
—Lady Mary Wortley Montagu

You teach people who you are by the way you treat yourself.
—Lynn Pierce, Author, "Change One Thing, Change Your Life"
www.ChangeOneThing.com

Kindness consists in loving people more than they deserve.
—Jacqueline Schiff

Kind words can be short and easy to speak,
but their echoes are truly endless.
—Mother Teresa

Let no one ever come to you without leaving better and happier.
Be the living expression of God's kindness: kindness in your face,
kindness in your eyes, kindness in your smile.
—Mother Teresa

Who practices hospitality entertains God Himself.
—Unknown

No one who achieves success does so without acknowledging the help of
others. The wise and confident acknowledge this help with gratitude.
— Unknown

Laughter

If you can laugh at it, you can live with it.
—Erma Bombeck

Time spent laughing is time spent with the Gods.
—Japanese Proverb

The best blush to use is laughter: It puts roses in your cheeks and in your soul.
—Linda Knight

Laughter opens places in us that are locked down.
Laughter is a whole body and whole soul experience.
In laughing we are less attached to what we think we know, making room
for fresh points of view and light heartedness. Our bodies quiver and shake
from the inside out, releasing tension and nudging us into new postures,
new attitudes. Laughter heals because laughter makes us whole.
It breaks down the barriers of our significance, our seriousness,
and our self-control. Laughter leaps like so many playful lambs over the
fence lines of our carefully constructed personas and connects us to
greener pastures in ourselves and others.
—Mary Manin Morrissey, Author "Life Keys"

The best person to laugh at is yourself.
Let others join in with you, and you'll find that the opinions of others
will no longer be a threat.
—Kay Presto, Speaker, Author "Create the Magic in YOUR Life"
Contributor to "Chicken Soup for the NASCAR Soul"

Blessed is she who has learned to laugh at herself for
she shall never cease to be entertained.
—Unknown

Leadership

The day will come when man will recognize woman as his peer,
not only at the fireside, but in councils of the nation.
Then, and not until then, will there be the perfect comradeship,
the ideal union between the sexes that shall result in the
highest development of the race.
—Susan B. Anthony

Could and should do little good.
When we teach by showing, we encourage growing.
—Cynthia Brian, speaker, radio and TV show host
Author of "Chicken Soup for the Gardener's Soul"
www.star-style.com, www.bethestaryouare.org

Each event in our lives and each experience that we have helps us get to the
next one. The important thing is to learn from them and go on from there.
—Liz Fetter, President and CEO, QRS Corporation
Excerpt from interview "Playing with the Big Boys" by Debra Pestrak
www.MostPowerfulWomen.com

A candle loses nothing by lighting another candle.
—Erin Majors

Leadership has been defined as many things, but the mark of a leader?
The mark of a true leader is one who can lead him/herself and MOVE —
take that first small step across a giant chasm. Action is the key!
On your way then!
—Gail Rosenthal, Consultant, Trainer

Dare to share your voice and be heard.
—Alexandra Sagerman, Speaking Coach, Actress
www.SpeakingPower.com

To impact an individual is inspiring,
but to inspire a leader multiplies your impact.
—Jennifer Rousseau Sedlock
www.JenniferSpeaks.com

Do not wait for leaders. Do it alone, person to person.
—Mother Teresa

Leaders understand the power of choice.
—Unknown

Efficiency tends to deal with Things.
Effectiveness tends to deal with People.
We manage things, we lead People.
—Unknown

Outstanding leaders appeal to the hearts of their followers —
not their minds.
—Unknown

The best leader is the one who has the sense to surround herself with
outstanding people and self-restraint not to meddle with how they do
their jobs.
—Unknown

Be ENTHUSIASTIC as a leader.
You can't light a fire with a wet match!
—Unknown

Enthusiasm will be as contagious as ever.
—Unknown

Life

Any day ABOVE ground is a GOOD Day!
—Advertising slogan for a cemetery

Life is not measured by the number of breaths we take
but by the moments that take our breath away.
—Anonymous

Some people go through life trying to find out what the world holds for them
only to find out too late that it's what they bring to the world that really counts.
OR It's not what the world holds for you it's what you bring to it.
—Anne of Green Gables

You have to do what you love to do, not get stuck in that comfort zone of a
regular job. Life is not a dress rehearsal. This is it.
—Lucinda Basset

It is not how many years we live, but rather what we do with them.
—Cory Booth, Evangeline

The essential conditions of everything you do must be choice, love, passion.
—Nadia Boulanger

Your day is going to happen whether you're happy about it or not.
—Karen Brady, Whatever/Whenever Supervisor, W Hotel

The rules of a happy life are these: Smile, Have Fun, and Be wild and Crazy.
Risk ridicule and enjoy the moment.
—Cynthia Brian, speaker, radio and TV show host
Author of "Chicken Soup for the Gardener's Soul"
www.bethestaryouare.org

Beginnings are scary. Endings are usually sad,
but it's the middle that counts the most.
—Sandra Bullock, from the movie "Hope Floats"

Life would be so much easier if we just had the source code.
—Bumper Sticker

Sometimes I wish life had subtitles.
—Bumper Sticker

A joyful life is a delicate balance of letting go of those things that
no longer serve us and embracing all the things that do.
—Beth Burns, Professional Life Coach
www.BrightSideCoaching.com

Life itself is the proper binge.
—Julia Child

Create a vision of the life you want to create - make it so clear and so vivid
that when you close your eyes you see it on the inside of your eyelids.
That vision will pull you forward and the steps you must take to make it
your reality will magically appear.
—Rebecca Everett, Speaker, Coach

I don't want life to imitate art.
I want life to be art.
—Carrie Fisher

LIVE WELL, LAUGH OFTEN!!!
—Peri C. Kalar

A life lived in chaos is an impossibility . . .
—Madeleine L'Engle

Real women don't have hot flashes.
They have power surges.
—Christine Mansfield

I've gone through life believing in the strength and competence of others,
never in my own. Now, dazzled, I discover that my capacities are real.
It's like finding a fortune in the lining of an old coat.
—Joan Mills

Bring love into this day. The present moment is all we have, and all we will ever
have, and it is where we find the joy and power of God's presence.
—Mary Manin Morrissey, Author "Life Keys"

You are more than your physical body-you are an energetic being.
—Caroline Myss

The good, the bad, hardship, joy, tragedy, love, and happiness are all
interwoven into one indescribable whole that one calls life. You cannot
separate the good from the bad, and perhaps there is no need to do so.
—Jacqueline Bouvier Kennedy Onassis

You're painting the canvas called your life.
How do you want it to look?
—Aleta Pippin, abstract painter and entrepreneur
Founder - A. Pippin's Art with Heart
Author - "Yikes! My Butt's Falling . . . Humorous 'Tails' of Baby Boomers
Searching for the Meaning of Life"

Don't sacrifice your life to work and ideals.
The most important things in life are human relations.
I found that out too late.
—Katharinde Susannah Prichard, Australian Author

Live today for tomorrow it will all be history.
—Proverb

While we have the gift of life, it seems to me the only tragedy
is to allow part of us to die whether it is our spirit,
our creativity or our glorious uniqueness.
—Gilda Radner

Life must be lived and curiosity kept alive.
—Eleanor Roosevelt

Variety is the spice of life.
—Beverly J. Roush

Yesterday is a dream, tomorrow but a vision.
But today well lived makes every yesterday a dream of happiness,
and every tomorrow a vision of hope. Look well, therefore to this day.
—Sanskrit Proverb

Life doesn't mean much when your happiness is based on the accumulation
of "things". Things can disappear in a flash. Then what do you have left?
You cannot be a saint in one area of your life and a sinner in another.
Life is the totality of your being.
--Heshie Segal, Speaker, Founder-The Girlfriend Connection
www.JetNettingConnection.com

Parents learn a lot from their children about coping with life.
—Muriel Spark

Life is a gift not something God owes us.
—Joni Wilson, Voice Expert, Author "Thunder Behind the Silence:
When a Woman Finds Her Voice"
www.JoniWilsonVoice.com

Often people attempt to live their lives backwards:
they try to have more things, or more money, in order to do more of what
they want so that they will be happier. The way it actually works is the reverse…
you must first BE who you really are, then DO what you need to do,
in order to HAVE what you want.
—Margaret Young

Love

Love is patient, love is kind. It does not envy, it does not boast, it is not proud. It is not rude, it is not self-seeking, it is not easily angered, it keeps no record of wrongs. Love does not delight in evil but rejoices with the truth. It always protects, always trusts, always perseveres. Love never fails. But where there are prophecies, they will cease; where there are tongues, they will be stilled; where there is knowledge, it will pass away . . . And now these things remain: faith, hope and love. But the greatest of these is love.
—1 Corinthians 13:1-8, 13

God,
I read the bible. What does begat mean? Nobody will tell me.
Love, Alison
Kid's Theology

Love is that condition in the human spirit so profound that it allows me to survive, and better than that, to thrive with passion, compassion, and style.
—Maya Angelou, American poet, writer, and actress

Love involves a peculiar unfathomable combination of understanding and misunderstanding.
—Diane Arbus

What the world really needs is more love and less paperwork.
—Pearl Bailey

I believe you must first learn to love and accept yourself unconditionally. Then you can truly love and accept someone else.
—Patrice Baker, Speaker, www.PowerOfWords.com

Feeling Love is like being on a diving board -
If you relax, let go, and enjoy the fall,
then soon you will be floating in a pool
of warmth, solitude and weightlessness.
—Patrice Carington, Speaker

You can give without loving, but you cannot love without giving.
—Amy Carmichael

Every day I live I am more convinced that the waste of life lies in the love
we have not given, the powers we have not used, the selfish prudence that
will risk nothing and which, shirking pain, misses happiness as well.
—Mary Cholmondeley

You can't put a price tag on love, but you can on all its accessories.
—Melanie Clark

It's love if they order one of those desserts that are on fire.
They like to order those because it's just like how their hearts are — on fire.
—Christine, age 9

Everyone has inside of him a piece of good news.
The good news is that you don't know how great you can be!
How much you can love! What you can accomplish!
And what your potential is!
—Anne Frank, 1929-1945, Jewish Refugee and Diarist

Love is the great miracle cure.
Loving ourselves works miracles in our lives.
—Louise L. Hay, Author "You Can Heal Your Life"

The truth is that there is only one terminal dignity — love.
And the story of a love is not important — what is important is that one is
capable of love. It is perhaps the only glimpse we are permitted of eternity.
—Helen Hayes

It really is worth fighting for, being brave for, risking everything for.
And the trouble is, if you don't risk everything, you risk even more.
—Erica Jong

Thru mysterious means, love travels... into closed hearts and opens them.
Eventually.
—Cath Kachur, Speaker, Artist
ww.HumanTuneUp.com

Love is always present, it is just a matter of feeling it or not.
—Kimberly Kirberg

Start living now. Stop saving the good china for that special occasion.
Stop withholding your love until that special person materializes.
Every day you are alive is a special occasion. Every minute, every breath,
is a gift from God.
—Mary Manin Morrissey, Author "Life Keys"

Love cannot make its home in a place where it's not invited.
Move into a practice which invites that Presence to make Its home in you
because it is home to that Presence. As you would with someone you love,
prepare a place of peace and comfort inside your heart, and Love finds
Its home right where you are.
—Mary Manin Morrissey, Author "Life Keys"

How can you tell if two adults eating dinner at a restaurant are in love?
Romantic adults usually are all dressed up, so if they are just wearing jeans it
might mean they used to go out or they just broke up.
—Sarah, age 9

Give God full permission.
—Mother Teresa

Love is a fruit in season at all times, and within reach of every hand.
—Mother Teresa

Dear God,
I bet it's very hard for you to love all of everybody in the whole world.
There are only 4 people in our family and I can never do it.
—Nan
"Kid's Theology"

Love is a friendship caught on fire.
—Northern Exposure, television series

I'm not rushing into being in love.
I'm finding fourth grade hard enough.
—Regina, age 10

Love is a gift of one's inner-most soul to another so both can be whole.
—Tea Rose

There is nothing more important in life than love.
—Barbra Streisand

To love is to receive a glimpse of heaven.
—Karen Sunde

Love is like a butterfly, hold it too tight, it'll crush,
hold it too loose, it'll fly.
—Unknown

The best way to love is to love like you have never been hurt.
—Unknown

Miracles occur naturally as expressions of love.
The real miracle is the love that inspires them.
In this sense everything that comes from love is miracle.
—Marianne Williamson, Author "A Woman's Worth"

Making a Difference

The area where we are the greatest is the area in which we inspire,
encourage, and connect with another human being.
—Maya Angelou, American poet, writer, and actress

When you tell someone that who they are makes a difference—they do!
—Helice "the Spark" Bridges, Author, "Who I Am Makes A Difference"
Founder and President, Difference Makers International

We must not, in trying to think about how we can make a big difference,
ignore the small daily differences we can make which, over time,
add up to big differences that we often cannot foresee.
—Marian Wright Edelman, Lobbyist on Behalf of Children

If you have knowledge, let others light their candles in it.
—Margaret Fuller

Those who are lifting the world upward and onward
are those who encourage more than criticize.
—Elizabeth Harrison

Enthusiasm is at the heart of any positive change in the world. Each of us have
something to offer to uplift the spirit of others, whether through achieving a
lifelong goal that inspires children to make better choices, influencing friends
to a healthier way of life, helping people heal themselves, creating a joyful
workplace or home, or connecting more deeply with family, nature, or a cause.
In all of its expressions, enthusiasm is a gift to be shared with the world.
Enthusiasm, however you define it, is at the core of all success. Whether you're
hoping to achieve a big dream, heal your body, find peace of mind, influence a
client to choose your product, push for a promotion, derive more pleasure from
your community or church, or have deeper committed relationships with those
you love, enthusiasm can help.
—Mary Marcdante, Speaker, Author "Living with Enthusiasm
www.MaryMarcdante.com

It's a great satisfaction knowing that for a brief point in time
you made a difference.
—Irene Natividad

Women are the real architects of society.
—Harriet Beecher Stowe

In politics, if you want anything said, ask a man;
if you want anything done, ask a woman.
—Margaret Thatcher

We can do no great things, only small things with great love.
—Mother Theresa

If you think you're too small to make a difference,
you've obviously never been in bed with a mosquito.
—Michelle Walker

The true stewardship of a woman lies not in what she has,
but in how she affects the lives of others.
—Rheba Washington-Lindsey, Author "Teaching Isn't For Cowards"

With every deed you are sowing a seed,
though the harvest you may not see.
—Ella Wheeler Wilcox

In every community, there is work to be done.
In every nation, there are wounds to heal.
In every heart, there is the power to do it.
—Marianne Williamson

To the world you might be one person,
but to one person you might be the world.
—Unknown

Sparkle-Tudes!

Marriage

Husbands are awkward things to deal with;
even keeping them in hot water will not make them tender.
—Mary Buckley

The trouble with some women is that they get all excited about nothing —
and then marry him.
—Cher

Do let him read the papers. But not while you accusingly tiptoe around the room, or perch much like a silent bird of prey on the edge of your most uncomfortable chair. (He will read them anyway, and he should read them, so let him choose his own good time.) Don't make a big exit. Just go.
But kiss him quickly, before you go, otherwise he might think you are angry; he is used to suspecting he is doing something wrong.
—Marlene Dietrich

Whatever you may look like, marry a man your own age —
as your beauty fades, so will his eyesight.
—Phyllis Diller

The kind of marriage you make depends upon the kind of person you are. If you are a happy, well-adjusted person, the chances are your marriage will be a happy one. If you have made adjustments so far with more satisfaction than distress, you are likely to make your marriage and family adjustments satisfactorily. If you are discontented and bitter about your lot in life, you will have to change before you can expect to live happily ever after.
—Evelyn Duvall, "When You Marry"

Husbands are like fires. They go out when unattended.
—Zsa Zsa Gabor

The more you invest in a marriage, the more valuable it becomes.
—Amy Grant

If you want to sacrifice the admiration of many men for the criticism of one,
go ahead, get married.
—Katharine Hepburn

Successful marriage is always a triangle: a man, a woman, and God.
—Cecil Myers

When Dolly Parton was asked by Melissa Etheridge on Oprah,
"Do you believe in same-sex marriages?"
Dolly replied, "Hell yes! Why shouldn't you folks have the
same tough times we go through!"

After marriage, a woman's sight becomes so keen that she can see right
through her husband without looking at him, and a man's so dull that he
can look right through his wife without seeing her.
—Helen Rowland

When a girl marries, she exchanges the attentions of all the other men
of her acquaintance for the inattention of just one.
—Helen Rowland

I think men who have a pierced ear are better prepared for marriage.
They've experienced pain and bought jewelry.
—Rita Rudner

Someone once asked me why women don't gamble as much as men do
and I gave the commonsensical reply that we don't have as much money.
That was a true but incomplete answer. In fact, women's total instinct for
gambling is satisfied by marriage.
—Gloria Steinem

Some pray to marry the man they love, my prayer will somewhat vary;
I humbly pray to Heaven above that I love the man I marry.
—Rose Pastor Stokes

The middle years of marriage are the most crucial. In the early years,
spouses want each other and in late years, they need each other.
—Rebecca Tilly

Adam and Eve had an ideal marriage.
He didn't have to hear about all the men she could have married,
and she didn't have to hear about the way his mother cooked.
—Unknown

A marriage is a series of friendships. Love serves as its underlying theme.
Friendships provide it with the new challenges around which the relationship
further develops.
—Unknown

The man who says his wife can't take a joke forgets that she took him.
—Unknown

One advantage of marriage it seems to me—
Is that when you fall out of love with him
Or he falls out of love with you
It keeps you together until maybe you fall in again.
—Judith Viorst

We all have a childhood dream that when there is love,
everything goes like silk, but the reality is that marriage
requires a lot of compromise.
—Raquel Welch

Don't show a man everything you can do
because you'll end up doing it the rest of your life.
—Helen Westort

Men & Relationships

Ever notice how all of women's problems start with men?
MENtal illness, MENstrual cramps, MENtal breakdown, MENopause.
And when we have real problems, it's HIS-terectomy!
Don't forget the "GUY" necologist!
-Anonymous

Man forgives woman anything save the wit to outwit him.
—Minna Antrim

If you want to catch something, running after it isn't always the best way.
—Lois McMaster Bujold

PRINCESS, HAVING HAD SUFFICIENT EXPERIENCE WITH PRINCES,
SEEKS FROG
—Bumper Sticker

If men are from Mars, then why can't we send them back?
—Bumper Sticker

I never married because there was no need.
I have three pets at home which answer the same purpose as a husband.
I have a dog which growls every morning, a parrot which swears all afternoon
and a cat that comes home late at night.
—Marie Corelli

You don't develop courage by being happy in your relationships everyday.
You develop it by surviving difficult times and challenging adversity.
—Barbara De Angelis

I know for me the subject of how to be in a relationship is precious and complicated and challenging. It wouldn't be right to make it look too easy.
—Helen Hunt, on her approach to TV Series, "Mad About You"

A man's got to do what a man's got to do. A woman must do what he can't.
—Rhonda Hansome

Women, when seeking a long term partnership, take up a daily practice of writing, walking, or foot massage to feel a strong connection to your spiritual self. Feeding yourself will keep the fullness of your life vibrant!
—JoAnn Marini, Relationship Coach, Author "Smart & Savvy Dater's Know..."
www.MorethanAmour.com

The test of man is how well he is able to feel about what he thinks.
The test of a woman is how well she is able to think about what she feels.
—Mary Mcdowell

Let us go forth together on this path called relationship,
side-by-side, hand-in-hand. Let us walk as equals, as one spirit.
—Sheryl Roush, Speaker, Author, www.SparklePresentations.com

A successful man is one who makes more money than his wife can spend.
A successful woman is one who can find such a man.
—Lana Turner

Men never remember, but women never forget.
—Unknown

—The five most essential words for a healthy, vital relationship are,
"I apologize" and "you are right."
—Unknown

If he says that you are too good for him - believe him.
—Unknown

Mid-Life for Women

Mid-life is when the growth of hair on our legs slows down.
This gives us plenty of time to care for
our newly acquired mustache.

Mid-life is when you go for a mammogram
and you realize that this is the only time someone
will ask you to appear topless.

In mid-life your memory starts to go.
In fact the only thing we can retain is water.

Mid-life means that you become more reflective . . .
You start pondering the "big" questions.

"What is life?"
"Why am I here?"

"How much Healthy Choice ice cream can I eat
before it's no longer a healthy choice?"

Miracles

Miracles happen when your inner desires push past the logical limitations of your understanding.
—Perry A, Author "People Are Just Desserts"
www.PerryA.com

I don't believe in miracles.
I rely on them!
—Bumper Sticker

God is a character, a real and consistent being, or He is nothing.
If God did a miracle He would deny His own nature and the universe would simply blow up, vanish, become nothing.
— Joyce Cary

For the truly faithful, no miracle is necessary.
For those who doubt, no miracle is sufficient.
—Nancy Gibbs

As you expand into your huge self, your attention moves away from lack and onto abundance, away from grievance and onto gratitude. Your heart opens up and you take in the wonder of the "little things" in life. Your eyes begin to see the miracles of life that surround you, and you stand in awe, in humble recognition. Your mind stops racing and you begin to just be here—soaking up the delight of the moment. You become a lover of life.
—Peggy O'Neill, Speaker, Author "Walking Tall:Overcoming Inner Smallness No Matter What Size You Are"
Small Miracles Unlimited, www.YoPeggy.com

Those occurrences called hocus-pocus, 'airy-fairy-woo-woo' or just plain nonsense by some are simply scientifically explainable events yet to be discovered.
—Sally Scobey, Author "Treasures from the Deep: What I Always Wanted to Tell My Child"

Money

There are people who have money and people who are rich.
—Coco Chanel

Money isn't everything... but it ranks right up there with oxygen.
—Rita Davenport

Net-worth and self-worth. Often confused.
—Cath Kachur, Speaker, Artist
www.HumanTuneUp.com

83% of us fret about money.
—Bernice Kanner, Author "Are You Normal?"

Money doesn't care who has it.
—Ann Landers

If you want greater prosperity in your life, start forming a vacuum to receive it.
—Catherine Ponder, Author "The Dynamic Laws of Prosperity"

Live on less, invest the rest.
—Beulah Underwood, Ph.D., Author, "A Paycheck Away from Poverty"

Begin now to tell your dollars where to go.
—Ginita Wall, CPA, CFP

Mothers

A mother's love for her child is like nothing else in the world.
It knows no law, no pity, it dares all things and crushes down remorselessly
all that stands in its path.
—Agatha Christie

When I was a teenager, I recall struggling with my identity and my self-worth.
There were many times that I came home and cried on my bed. Boys made
fun of me, and called me names. There were numerous times I felt ugly and
worthless. I will never forget the gift of you! The beautiful words you shared
with me. You kept telling me not to pay attention to such nonsense, and how
beautiful and special I was. You forever gave me strength, love, courage and
passion. Your support and love are in my heart forever. I love forever, with
every fiber of my being.
—Lisa R. Delman, Author "Letters from the Heart,"
To My Mother: A Daughter's Voice
www.HeartfeltMatters.com

A mother understands what a child does not say.
—Jewish Saying

The phrase "working mother" is redundant.
—Jane Sellman

Children are the sum of what mothers contribute to their lives.
—Unknown

Of all the rights of women, the greatest is to be a mother.
—Lin Yü-tang

Poetry is music written for the human voice.
—Maya Angelou, American poet, writer, and actress

It had never occurred to me before that music and thinking are so much alike.
In fact you could say music is another way of thinking, or maybe thinking is
another kind of music.
—Ursula K. Le Guin

Music:
To the deaf -- it is the heartbeat of movement,
To the hearing -- it is the voice of GOD,
To the musician who plays the finite instrument --
it is an expression of passion, and
To a mother -- it is the breath of her child and hearing them laughing.
—Mona M. Mordoff, Speaker, Writer

Music is the soul's desire to sing.
—Sheryl Roush, Speaker, Author Sparkle-Tudes!
www.SparklePresentations.com

Every single one of us can do things that no one else can do —
can love things that no one else can love. We are like violins.
We can be used for doorstops, or we can make music.
You know what to do.
—Barbara Sher

Nature

If we had no winter, the spring would not be so pleasant: if we did not sometimes taste of adversity, prosperity would not be so welcome.
Anne Bradstreet, 1612-1672, Poet

Dear God,
I didn't think orange went with purple until I saw the sunset you made on Tuesday night. That was really cool.
—Carol
"Kid's Theology"

The power of nature to calm, heal and inspire
is enormous for those that take the time to look.
The flaming clouds of a summer sunset;
the buttercup yellow of a full moon rising on a cloudless night;
mist sweeping up a valley;
bird calls at dawn,
all lift me beyond the present,
even if sometimes only for a moment.
—Anne Frodsham, horticulturist and nature lover

Dear God,
Did you mean for giraffes to look like that or was it an accident?
—Norma
"Kid's Theology"

Go outside.
Leave the sidewalks behind.
—Cath Kachur, Speaker, Artist
ww.HumanTuneUp.com

Snowflakes are one of Nature's most fragile things,
but just look what they can do when they stick together.
—Verna Kelley

Like water, be gentle and strong.
Be gentle enough to follow the natural paths of the earth,
and strong enough to rise up and reshape the world.
—Brenda Peterson

Nature is beautiful.
It is the basis of our survival.
No nature, no us.
—Alison J. Roush, 8 years old and the saviour of all things living.

Even when the desert is quiet, the sands sing.
—Sheryl Roush, speaker, author Sparkle-Tudes!
www.SparklePresentations.com

There is a wonderful law of nature that the three things
we crave most - happiness, freedom, and peace of mind-
are always attained by giving them to someone else.
—Unknown

The more we are separated from nature,
the unhappier we get.
—Unknown

You can't get much closer to God than this!
—Wardene Weisser, nature photographer

Opportunity

If you are waiting to get discovered on your merit alone - Forget it!
You must act on opportunities to allow others to discover YOU.
—Debbie Allen, Speaker, Author "Confessions of Shameless Self Promoters"
www.DebbieAllen.com

Too often the opportunity knocks,
but by the time you push back the chain,
push back the bolt,
unhook the locks
and shut off the burglar alarm,
it's too late.
—Rita Coolidge

When the sun rises, it rises for everyone.
—Cuban Proverb

The sad truth is that opportunity doesn't knock twice.
You can put things off until tomorrow but tomorrow may never come.
Where will you be a few years down the line.
Will it be everything you dreamed of.
We seal our fate with the choices we take,
but don't give a second thought to the chances we take.
—Gloria Estefan

Sometimes only a change of viewpoint is needed to convert a tiresome
duty into an interesting opportunity.
—Alberta Flanders

An opportunity is a terrible thing to waste.
—- Anita Jefferson

Great opportunities to help others seldom come,
but small ones surround us daily.
—Sally Koch

Opportunities are usually disguised as hard work,
so most people don't recognize them.
—Ann Landers

One can present people with opportunities.
One cannot make them equal to them.
—Rosamond Lehmann

Another key to success is having the ability and willingness to open the door
that someone else hasn't yet opened. Turn things upside down and think
about them differently. Take things apart and put them back together again.
—Anne Sweeney, President, Disney/ABC Cable Networks and
President, Disney Channel
Excerpt from interview "Playing with the Big Boys" by Debra Pestrak
www.MostPowerfulWomen.com

Doors of opportunity don't open, they unlock;
it is up to you to turn the knob.
—Lily Taylor

People think that at the top there isn't much room.
They tend to think of it as an Everest.
My message is that there is tons of room at the top.
—Margaret Thatcher

Opportunities can drop in your lap . . .
if you place your lap where opportunities drop.
—Unknown

Opportunities are never lost; they are taken by others.
—Unknown

Optimism

Some people are still unaware that reality contains unparalleled beauties.
The fantastic and unexpected, the ever-changing and renewing is nowhere
so exemplified as in real life itself.
—Berenice Abbott

Like a diamond, and in life, some of the facets are dark.
But the light reflects off those facets and bounces back through the
diamond with great brilliance.
—Eln Albert, Speaker, Author

Still, when it looked like the sun wasn't going to shine anymore,
God put a rainbow in the clouds.
—Maya Angelou, American poet, writer, and actress

I could never be cynical, not that I think there's anything wrong with cynicism.
I think it can be quite funny at times. But I just feel so grateful to be alive.
—Drew Barrymore, Actress

An optimist is the human personification of spring.
—Susan J. Bissonette

Make the most with what you have, and be happy with it.
—Rosemary Burnham

My quest is ultimate positivity—spreading it and helping others feel it.
—Ms. Dynamite, Teen People, 2003

I don't think of all the misery, but of all the beauty that still remains.
—Anne Frank

In The Land of I Can, there are no barriers - no limitations.
The words, "I Can't," do not exist.
—Susan L. Gilbert, Speaker, Author "The Land of I Can"
www.SusanGilbert.com   www. UnityProducts.com

No pessimist ever discovered the secrets of the stars or sailed to an
uncharted land or opened a new heaven to the human spirit.
—Helen Keller

Discover the best in yourself and you'll discover the best in everything else.
—Mary Marcdante, Speaker, Author of "Living with Enthusiasm"
www.MaryMarcdante.com

Is the cup half full or half empty? It doesn't matter. I have a glass.
That means I'm in the game of life and life can change at any moment.
--Stephanie Moles, www.TheWoman'sHeart.org

I shut my eyes and all the world drops dead;
I lift my eyes and all is born again.
—Sylvia Plath

I am optimistic and confident in all that I do.
I affirm only the best for myself and others.
I am the creator of my life and my world.
I meet daily challenges gracefully and with complete confidence.
I fill my mind with positive, nurturing, and healing thoughts.
—Alice Potter, Author "The Positive Thinker, I Can Do That!"
and "Putting the Positive Thinker to Work: 21 Ways and 21 Days
to a Happy Fulfilling, Successful Life"

Originality

Know that when you follow your heart's desire
everything else for everyone else is in Divine order.
—Perry A, Author "People Are Just Desserts"
www.PerryA.com

One of the things that has made me successful over time and not only in work
but in most of my dealings, is that pretty consistently, what you see is who I am.
—Ursula Burns, Vice President Worldwide Manufacturing Operations, Xerox
Excerpt from interview "Playing with the Big Boys" by Debra Pestrak
www.MostPowerfulWomen.com

True power is being able to affect the world with who we are.
—Patrice Carington

In order to be irreplaceable one must always be different.
—Coco Chanel

Make the choice to be your highest and best self,
regardless of the circumstances.
—Rosalene Glickman, Ph.D., Author "Optimal Thinking"
www.OptimalThinking.com

Each one of us has a contribution to make and a legacy to leave.
We all have at least one person who needs what we have to offer.
How easily we forget this in the middle of a busy day or a personal crisis.
How much we need to remember this! You are precious, unrepeatable gift to
the world. Unwrap yourself. The world is waiting for you.
—Mary Marcdante, Speaker, Author "Living with Enthusiasm:
How the 21-Day Smile Diet Can Change Your Life"
www.MaryMarcdante.com

We are each a once-in-a-universe kind of being.
Bring Honor to that which is sacred —
the Higher Power that reveals Itself to us—
by taking the next step that has been given.
—Mary Manin Morrissey, Author "Life Keys"

Your Being is an unfathomable mystery of wonder and beauty.
Turn your gaze inward and see what is there. Then, honor that Being.
—Peggy O'Neill, Speaker, Author "Walking Tall:Overcoming Inner Smallness
No Matter What Size You Are"
Small Miracles Unlimited, www.YoPeggy.com

Remember always that you have not only a right to be an individual,
you have an obligation to be one. You cannot make any useful contribution
in life unless you do this.
—Eleanor Roosevelt

Reflect your brilliance!
—Sheryl Roush, speaker, author Sparkle-Tudes!
www.SparklePresentations.com

You are the product of your own brainstorm.
—Rosemary Konner Steinbaum

I believe that you need to plant yourself where you'll bloom,
rather than trying to bloom where you're planted.
—Jean E. Walker, Author of Age Advantage

The God that gives us life gives us the tools for our expansion and is not
responsible for how we use those tools.
—Joni Wilson, Voice Expert, Author "Thunder Behind the Silence:
When a Woman Finds Her Voice"
www.JoniWilsonVoice.com

Overcoming Adversity

You never know what events are going to transpire to get you home.
—From the movie "Apollo 13"

When you come to a roadblock, take a detour.
—Mary Kay Ash

No pressure, no diamonds.
—Mary Case

A gem cannot be polished without friction, nor a man perfected without trials.
—Chinese Proverb

What I am looking for is a blessing not in disguise.
—Kitty O'Neill Collins

You don't develop courage by being happy in your relationships everyday.
You develop it by surviving difficult times and challenging adversity.
—Barbara De Angelis

Blessed are the flexible for they shall not be bent out of shape.
—Cath Kachur, Speaker, Artist

Every obstacle we encounter is a natural and necessary step
on the road to achieving our dreams.
—Cynthia Kersey, Speaker, Author "Unstoppable" www.unstoppable.net

People are like stained — glass windows. They sparkle and shine when the sun
is out, but when the darkness sets in, their true beauty is revealed only if there is
a light from within.
—Elizabeth Kubler-Ross

Turn your face to the sun and the shadows fall behind you
—Maori Proverb

Stumbling is not falling.
—Portuguese Proverb

No matter how much you're struggling today, always look to tomorrow.
Then you will look back and realize you can always, manage whatever life
brings you.
—Joanne Roush

Every blade of grass has its angel that bends over it and whispers, grow, grow.
—The Talmud

The difference between stumbling blocks and stepping stones is how you use
them.
— Unknown

The stars are constantly shining, but often we do not see them until the dark
hours.
— Unknown

Two frogs fell into a bowl of cream. One didn't panic, he relaxed and drowned.
The other kicked and struggled so much that the cream turned to butter and he
walked out.
— Unknown

We need tough days to drive us to our knees.
— Unknown

Always continue the climb. It is possible for you to do whatever you choose, if
you first get to know who you are and are willing to work with a power that is
greater than ourselves to do it.
—Oprah Winfrey

Parenting

I only give advice to my children when they ask for it
and they pay me.
--Iris Adam, Natural Law Party Candidate for Governor of California, 2002, 2003

You see much more of your children once they leave home.
—Lucille Ball, Comediene

We are spending our kids' inheritance.
—Bumper Sticker

Be nice to your kids. They'll choose your nursing home.
—Bumper Sticker

Don't expect your children to do
anything you won't do for yourself.
—Colette Carlson, Speaker
Contributing author, "Conversations on Success"
www.colettecarlson.com

There actually was a time I was a perfect parent and I knew all the answers —
then, the first baby came along and suddenly I realized I didn't even know
what the questions were.
—Rita Emmett - Recovering Procrastinator
Author "The Procrastinating Child: A Handbook for Adults to Help Children
Stop Putting Things Off"
www.RitaEmmett.com

People either imitate or make vows not to be like their parents.
—Cath Kachur, Speaker, Artist
www.HumanTuneUp.com

We need to teach the next generation of children from day one that they are responsible for their lives. Mankind's greatest gift, also its greatest curse, is that we have free choice. We can make our choices built from love or from fear.
—Elizabeth Kubler-Ross

It's never too late to be a better parent. Start today.
Model the behavior you wish to see in your children.
Discipline with wisdom and gentleness.
Love freely and openly, expressing often and in many ways how you cherish and value each of your children, just as God treasures each of us.
—Mary Manin Morrissey, Author "Life Keys"

Teach your children to choose the right path, and when they are older, they will remain upon it.
—Proverbs 22:6

Children are our second chance to have a great parent-child relationship.
—Dr. Laura Schlessinger

It doesn't matter who my father was;
it matters who I remember he was.
—Anne Sexton

Having kids—the responsibility of rearing good, kind, ethical, responsible human beings—the biggest job anyone can embark on. Like any risk, you have to take a leap of faith and ask lots of wonderful people for their help and guidance. I thank God everyday for giving me the opportunity to parent.
— Maria Kennedy Shriver Schwartzenegger

 Passion

Passion is a first kiss and a last.
Passion is a steaming "Cup of Joe."
Passion is entering the 10K — just because.
Passion is creating life in your likeness.
Passion is volunteering at the shelter.
Passion is loving the beach on an overcast day.
Passion is cradling a newborn kitten.
Passion is teaching a child to read the printed word.
Passion is placing a stroke of magenta on a white canvas.
Passion is not letting the cancer win.
Passion is listening to the same CD thirty times in a row.
Passion is noticing the smile on a stranger's face.
Passion is the next keystroke of an overdue letter.
Passion is discovering love after the infatuation.
Passion is fitting together the jigsaw of life.
—Lee A. Barron, Publisher, Author

I know your purpose in life — it's to live your very best life.
The real question is how are you going to do just that?
—Beth Burns, Professional Life Coach
www.BrightSideCoaching.com

Find something you're passionate about and
keep tremendously interested in it.
—Julia Child

My passion is my most effective talent.
My passion may also be my most dangerous weakness.
—Daniela Hiles, Top Sales Award Recipient
Sales/Catering Manager, Westin Los Angeles Airport

Finding your passion is connecting the dots between your head and your heart.
—Maria Marsala
www.ElevatingYou.com

Find what you have a passion for in life . Without it you will be going through your days always asking "Is there more?" By pursuing our passion we will be willing to persevere during the challenges to reach our dreams.
—Debra Pestrak, Speaker, Author "Playing with the Big Boys"
www.DebraPestrak.com

Passion is not only a feeling or individual emotion.
It is the abundant excitement of living life to its fullest.
—Sheryl Roush, Speaker "Perc-U-Lating Power:
The Magic of Having More Passion and Purpose in Life"
www.SparklePresentations.com

It is only by expressing all that is inside that purer and purer streams come.
—Brenda Ueland

Your true passion should feel like breathing; it's that natural.
—Oprah Winfrey

5 Steps to Finding Your Passion
From Oprah's Lifestyle Makeovers: How to Find Your Passion
Guest Cheryl Richardson, Author, Speaker

True happiness comes when you do what you are most passionate about. Uncover your true passion—and start living it!

1. Get Quiet

2. Become Sensitive to Your Environment

3. Answer a Series of Questions:
    What interest, passion or desire are you most afraid of
    admitting to yourself and others?
    What do you love about yourself?
    Who do you know that's doing something you'd like to do?
        Describe yourself doing it.
    How could you make the world a better place for yourself and others?
    What's stopping you from moving forward with exploring your passion?

4. Go on a Treasure Hunt

5. Take a Risk

**Today a new sun rises for me;
everything lives,
everything is animated,
everything seems to speak to me of my passion,
everything invites me to cherish it.
-- Anne de Lenclos --**

Now Begin

Beneath the degrees, titles, accomplishments,

What is inside, to be discovered at your core?

What is your unique and special spark?

Buried deep, neglected, chosen to ignore

Seeking to please whomever

Drowning out pure longings of your heart

Struggling, freezing, suffocating

Until finally, you choose to start

Whispers from the spirit

Souls songs from deep within

After dancing, stranger among strangers,

Claim it! Your life! Now begin!

—Julie Jordan Scott —
www.5passions.com

Patience

Pay attention.
Attend to patience.
—Iris Adam, Natural Law Party Candidate for Governor of California, 2002, 2003

Be patient.
God isn't finished with me yet.
—Bumper Sticker

Patience is the ability to idle your motor
when you feel like stripping your gears.
—Barbara Johnson

Patience [restraint of tongue and pen]
Dear God,
If I cannot answer yes to each one of these,
please grant me the strength to keep my lips closed
and my fingers off the keyboard:
1)   Does it need to be said?
2)   Is it the truth?
3)   Can it be said with love and kindness?
4)   Does it need to be said by me?
--Stephanie Moles, www.TheWoman'sHeart.org

"Call to me and I will answer you and tell you great and
unsearchable things you do not know," says the Lord.
—Jeremiah 33:3
Women's Devotional Bible 2, New International Version

If you are tempted to lose patience with others;
stop and think how patient God has been with you.
—Unknown

Peace

If you want a better world, become a better person.
—Lydia Boyd, Past International Director, Toastmasters International

Let there be peace on Earth; and let it begin with me.
—Song lyrics

Nonviolence is the supreme law of life.
—Indian Proverb

One little person, giving all of her time to peace, makes news.
Many people, giving some of their time, can make history.
—Peace Pilgrim

When you find peace within yourself, you become the kind of person
who can live at peace with others.
—Peace Pilgrim

Peace with a club in hand is war.
—Portuguese Proverb

If we want a free and peaceful world, if we want to make the deserts bloom
and man grow to greater dignity as a human being-we can do it.
—Eleanor Roosevelt

How can we have peace on the planet,
if we don't even have peace in our parking lots?
—Sheryl Roush, Speaker, Author
www.SparklePresentations.com

Everybody today seems to be in such a terrible rush, anxious for greater developments and greater riches and so on, so that children have very little time for their parents. Parents have very little time for each other, and in the home begins the disruption of peace of the world.
—Mother Teresa

Let us not be justices of the peace, but angels of peace.
—Saint Theresa of Lisieu

If a man would live in peace he should be blind, deaf, and dumb.
—Turkish Proverb

Peace is the deliberate adjustment of my life to the will of God.
—Unknown

There is nothing so lovely and enduring in the regions which surround us, above and below, as the lasting peace of a mind centered in God.
—Yoga Vasishtha

Perseverance

One of the things I learned the hard way was that it doesn't pay to get discouraged. Keeping busy and making optimism a way of life can restore your faith in yourself.
—Lucille Ball

We can do anything we want to do -- if we stick to it long enough.
—Helen Keller

It takes as long as it takes.
—Kathelen R. Johnson, www.TheTeachersVoice.com

When someone tells you that you can't go any farther,
just tell them to look behind you and see how far you've come.
—Lorna Pitre

God will do for me what I cannot do for myself.
But he will not do for me what I can do for myself - so get busy.
--Stephanie Moles, www.TheWoman'sHeart.org

Just do it — with class!
—Janet R. Stannard

You may have to fight a battle more than once to win it.
—Margaret Thatcher

Always continue the climb.
It is possible for you to do whatever you choose,
if you first get to know who you are
and are willing to work with a power that
is greater than ourselves to do it.
—Oprah Winfrey

Pessimism

Be kind to unkind people; they probably need it the most.
—Ashleigh Brilliant

Don't let negative people eat your positive karma.
—Yolanda Contreras, Supervisor, Sheraton Suites

Although the world is full of suffering,
it is also full of the overcoming of it.
— Helen Keller

Do you have relatives that do nothing but complain and criticize?
Don't let them get to you. God gave you two ears so things could go in
one ear and out the other. Use them.
—Kathy Laurenhue

The number one cause of inner smallness is that critical voice inside your head.
Pay attention. When you notice a thought is negative or cruel: defend yourself!
Silence that voice! Command it to STOP!
—Peggy O'Neill, Speaker, Author "Walking Tall: Overcoming Inner Smallness
No Matter What Size You Are"
Small Miracles Unlimited, www.YoPeggy.com

I doubt anyone will ever see—anywhere—a memorial to a pessimist.
—Unknown

All of us could take a lesson from the weather.
It pays no attention to criticism.
—Unknown

Possibilities

How far is far, how high is high?
We'll never know until we try.
—California Special Olympics, theme song

We are the painters of our own self-portraits and who we become,
next week, next year, or five years from now, will be determined by our
attitudes, our actions, and what we learn.
—Mary-Ellen Drummond, Speaker, Author
www.medrummond.com

We don't know who we are until we see what we can do.
—Martha Grimes

The words you speak have the power to transform the lives of others when
you speak words of encouragement, vision, opportunity and commitment.
—Donna Fisher, Speaker, Author "Communication Strategies that Work"

A flower grows out of a crack in the sidewalk . . . anything is possible.
—Cath Kachur, Speaker, Artist
www.HumanTuneUp.com

Positive expectations set in motion a course that allows you to tap into your
enthusiasm and access your deeper desires. Savor your positive expectations.
—Mary Marcdante, Speaker, Author "Living with Enthusiasm:
How the 21-Day Smile Diet Can Change Your Life"
www.MaryMarcdante.com

Something which we think is impossible now
is not impossible in another decade.
—Constance Baker Motley
(First Black Woman in the U.S. to become a Federal Judge)

I am willing to put myself through anything;
temporary pain or discomfort means nothing to me
as long as I can see that the experience will take me to a new level.
I am interested in the unknown, and the only path to the unknown
is through breaking barriers, an often-painful process.
—Diana Nyad

If you don't go after what you want, you'll never have it.
If you don't ask, the answer is always no.
If you don't step forward,
you're always in the same place.
—Nora Roberts

When you give yourself the permission to play-
it allows you to discover
and free
the creative visionary
you have within-
and experience
what might be possible.
—Alexandra Sagerman, Speaker, Actress, Author
"Unleash Your Speaking Power: Ten Essential Tips for
Powerful Delivery," www.SpeakingPower.com

Each of us is bound by our perceived limitations, but if we are open
to the possibility of a break through, we have the ability to significantly
enrich our lives.
--Heshie Segal, Speaker, Founder-The Girlfriend Connection
www.JetNettingConnection.com

If you only look at what is,
you might never attain what could be.
—Unknown

Some people see the possibilities in a problem - -
and some see the problems in a possibility.
—Donna Weiser, Discover Financial

Prayer

For the eyes of the Lord are on the righteous and
his ears are attentive to their prayer.
—I Peter 3:12
Women's Devotional Bible 2, New International Version

Life is fragile . . . handle with prayer.
—Bumper Sticker

There are three answers to prayers:
1) Yes
2) No
3) Wait
—Emily B. DeShazo

Sometimes the most important thing in a whole day is the rest we take
between two deep breaths, or the turning inward in prayer for five short
minutes.
—Etty Hillesum

I pray hard, work hard, and leave the rest to God.
—Florence "FloJo" Griffith Joyner, Olympian

Do not be anxious about anything, but in everything, by prayer and petition,
with thanksgiving, present your requests to God. And the peace of God,
which transcends all understanding, will guard your hearts and your minds
in Jesus Christ.
—Philippians 4:6-7
Women's Devotional Bible 2, New International Version

Ask God's blessing on your work, but don't ask him to do it for you.
—Dame Flora Robson

Thank God for this glorious day.
I shall rise, rejoice and be glad in it.
Thank you for every way in which I experience your Love -
through giving, sharing and receiving.
Use my life.
I am your messenger.
—Sheryl Roush, Speaker, Author

"Modeh Ani"
"I am grateful before you."
These are the first words you are to say in the morning in traditional Jewish life.
When you start the day being grateful, the hectic morning rush
(kids, dog, sandwiches, backpacks) falls into perspective...
(if you have a moment to think about it).
—Linda Kaplan Spitz, MD

Do not make prayer a monologue—make it a conversation.
—Unknown

God's answers are wiser than our prayers.
—Unknown

Five Fingers of Prayer

1. Your thumb is nearest to you. Begin your prayers by praying for those closest to you. They are the easiest to remember.

2. The next finger is the pointing finger. Pray for those who teach, instruct and heal. This includes teachers, doctors, and ministers. They need support and wisdom in pointing others in the right direction. Keep them in your prayers.

3. The next finger is the tallest finger. It reminds us of our leaders. Pray for the president, leaders in business and industry and administrators. These people shape our nation and guide public opinion. They need God's guidance.

4. The fourth finger is our ring finger. Surprising to many is the fact that this is our weakest finger, as any piano teacher will testify. It should remind us to pray for those who are weak, in trouble or in pain. They need your prayers day and night. You cannot pray too much for them.

5. And lastly comes our little finger; the smallest finger of all, which is where we should place ourselves in relation to God and others. As the Bible says, "The least shall be the greatest among you. The last shall be first." Your pinkie should remind you to pray for yourself. By the time you have prayed for the other four groups, your own needs will be put into proper perspective and you will be able to pray for yourself more effectively.

—Anonymous

My Daily Prayer

If I can do some good today,
If I can serve along life's way,
If I have something helpful say,
Lord, show me how.
If I can right a human wrong,
If I can help to make one strong,
If I can cheer with smile or song,
Lord, show me how.
If I can aid one in distress,
If I can make a burden less,
If I can spread more happiness,
Lord, show me how.

—Unknown —

The Woman's Prayer

Now I lay me

Down to sleep.

I pray the Lord

My shape to keep.

Please no wrinkles

Please no bags

Please lift my butt

Before it sags.

Please no age spots

Please no gray

And as for my belly,

Please take it away.

Please keep me healthy

Please keep me young,

And thank you Dear Lord

For all that you've done.

Amen

Pregnancy

Question & Answer:

Q: I'm two months pregnant now.
When will my baby move?

A: With any luck, right after he finishes college.

Q: My wife is five months pregnant and so moody that
sometimes she's borderline irrational.

A: So, what's your question?

Q: My childbirth instructor says it's not pain I'll feel during labor,
but pressure. Is she right?

A: Yes, in the same way that a tornado might be called an air current.

Q: When is the best time to get an epidural?

A: Right after you find out you're pregnant.

Q: Our baby was born last week.
When will my wife begin to feel and act normal again?

A: When the kids are in college.

Prosperity

I consider myself rich if I have health, wisdom and compassion.
—Debbie Bermont, Speaker, Author
www.SimplePrinciples.com

The best things in life aren't things.
—Bumper Sticker

If you want 1 year of prosperity, grow grain.
If you want 10 years of prosperity, grow trees.
If you want 100 years of prosperity, grow people.
—Chinese Proverb

Wealth grows in a grateful pocket.
The key to gathering wealth is, in all circumstances,
appreciating what you have.
—Terah Kathryn Collins, Author, Founder of the Western School of Feng Shui
www.wsfs.com

My friends are my estate.
—Emily Dickinson

If you have your health, love, some money and free time,
you are wealthy by definition.
—Cath Kachur, Speaker, Artist
www.HumanTuneUp.com

Every penny that I find, Helps me out of the daily grind. Every dollar towards my dream, Helps me build momentum and steam.
—Dianne Onstad, Co-author of "ABC's of YES! ~ Actions For Prosperity"
www.MagicOfYes.com

People can be rich, but that does not make them wealthy.
Wealthy people have learned balance in their relationships, spiritually, physically, emotionally and financially.
—Debra Pestrak, Speaker, Author "Playing with the Big Boys"
www.DebraPestrak.com

All prosperity begins in the mind and is dependent only upon the full use of our creative imagination.
—Ruth Ross

Prosperity is Divine love in action.
Prosperity is manifested through ideas on the physical level.
Prosperity is much more than money.
We are prosperous to the degree that we are experiencing love, peace, harmony, health and plenty in our life.
Money is spiritual, or spiritual energy.
—Sheryl Roush, Speaker, Author "Sparkle-Tudes!"
www.SparklePresentations.com

The real measure of your wealth is how much you'd be worth if you lost all your money.
—Unknown

The 8 Universal Laws of Prosperity:

1. Cleansing and Elimination – The first stage of creating prosperity is releasing. This may mean old patterns, thoughts, beliefs, losing weight, clothes, dust-collectors around the house, books, clutter, even relationships that no longer serve us.

2. Vacuum and Circulation – By releasing the old, we make space for the new, and better. A vacuum is then created to be filled back up again. Circulation begins again.

3. Order and Expansion – Only by having a sense of order and organization can there be an expansion. Clean up the clutter, get organization and be ready to receive more.

4. Forgiveness and Release – By forgiving those who we believe have done us wrong somehow, we release the negative energy from that experience or those people. Often the ones we truly need to forgive is ourselves. Through this forgiveness, we have a greater purity in our hearts, and less stress.

5. "Give-ability" and Tithing – Our ability to receive more is directly linked to our ability to give. We can offer our time, energy, talents, earnings, compassion . . . True giving is without any expectation of receiving.

6. Receptivity – With all this releasing, and giving, our hearts and lives are now ready to receive. The space is made available in our homes, work environments and hearts. By releasing old love relationships, we're ready to find new ones, fresh starts. By giving clothes away, our closets can hold more, newer styles and colors that make us feel better about ourselves.

7. Creativity – With fresh minds and environments, new ideas are inspired to grace us. Perhaps pursue a newfound inspiration for reading or writing new books, poetry, recipes, sport, gardening, crafts or hobbies.

8. Love – The law supports loving others, as best and as unconditionally as we are able. It may be through prayer for those we know need support, peace, condolences, or healing. By giving love first we receive it. It comes back to us from other sources, too.

These eight steps, or laws, enable us to receive, give and share more of the Universal love and Divine guidance in our lives, which attracts more prosperity.

—Sheryl Roush, Speaker, Author
www.SparklePresentations.com

Purpose

There is no duty as important as honoring your desire.
—Perry A, Author "People Are Just Desserts"
www.PerryA.com

Ah, but reach we must and it is then we may find the best
we might never imagine —reach.
—Lee A. Barron – Author

My passions were all gathered together like fingers that made a fist.
Drive is considered aggression today; I knew it then as purpose.
—Bette Davis

No matter what age you are, or what your circumstances might be,
you are special, and you still have something unique to offer.
Your life, because of who you are, has meaning.
—Barbara De Angelis

Take so many people to the middle of nowhere
that it becomes somewhere.
—Paulette Ensign, Author "How to Promote Your Business with Booklets"
www.TipsBooklets.com

When you're on purpose, life fits.
—Mary Marcdante, Speaker, Author "Living with Enthusiasm"
www.MaryMarcdante.com

Enthusiasm is more than showing excitement;
it is a gift from your Higher Power directing
and guiding you toward your life's purpose.
—Mary Marcdante, Speaker, Author "Living with Enthusiasm:
How the 21-Day Smile Diet Can Change Your Life"
www.MaryMarcdante.com

What if you embraced in your heart
that each person you encounter
is an equally magnificent creation?
That means that you are as valuable
as anyone else on the planet.
You have a specific, unique purpose and destiny.
From your core is a fountain or wellspring of possibilities.
All you need to do is to stay grounded and focused on your daily goal
or intention of a life in alignment with the calling of your life put into daily
actions reflecting those calling. You can do this. You are worth it.
You are big enough, strong enough, sure enough,
and have enough resources. Today! Here and Now!
—Julie Jordan Scott
www.5passions.com

Self-Acceptance

Love begins deep inside with self love.
We cannot get our self love outside, love cannot be created;
it simply is a state of being. Remembering this is the key.
—Linda Cammarata, RN, International musician, www.LifeCoaching.net

The minute you settle for less than you deserve,
you get even less than you settled for.
—Maureen Dowd

Accept that, quite possibly, you're exactly where you need to be
in your life right now.
—Cath Kachur, Speaker, Artist, www.HumanTuneUp.com

We are accountable only to ourselves
for what happens to us in our lives.
—Mildred Newman

Perfect is not what you try to be.
Perfect is what YOU already ARE.
—Laura Rubinstein, Coach, www.LBRandAssociates.com

Look at a day when you are supremely satisfied at the end.
It's not a day when you lounge around doing nothing;
it's when you've had everything to do, and you've done it.
—Margaret Thatcher, Former British Prime Minister

Seek not good from without:
seek it within yourselves, or you will never find it.
—Bertha Von Suttner

Self-Discovery

Obstacles are the struggling emergence of our hidden inner desires
seeking recognition.
—Perry A, Author "People Are Just Desserts"
www.PerryA.com

Independence is an invaluable trait.
It gives you confidence, freedom, and the ability to prosper
through anything life brings you.
—Natalie D. Brecher, CPM®, Speaker
Author of "Business without Biceps: The Untold Truths of Women in Business
and How to Make Them Work for You"

Life's lessons never end. A lesson is repeated until learned.
—Cath Kachur, Speaker, Artist
www.HumanTuneUp.com

I feel there is something unexplored about a woman
that only a woman can explore.
—Georgia O'Keeffe

Sometimes the best way to figure out who you are is to get to that place
where you don't have to be anything else.
—Unknown

Life is only about our own learning and if we travel the path in wisdom,
we will watch and observe the deeds of those around us and learn from
their mistrials thereby adding their lesson to our own experience bank.
—Joni Wilson, Voice Expert
Author "Thunder Behind the Silence: When a Woman Finds Her Voice"
www.JoniWilsonVoice.com

Self-Esteem

What would you do to someone if they talked to your children
the way you talk to yourself?
—A question to ponder

There are two things people want more than sex and money . . .
recognition and praise.
—Mary Kay Ash, Founder of Mary Kay Cosmetics

Love yourself first and everything else falls into line.
You have to really love yourself to get anything done in this world.
—Lucille Ball, Comedienne

Let the world know you as you are, not as you think you should be—
because sooner or later, if you are posing, you will forget the pose
and then where are you?
—Fanny Brice

When we let go of our investment in being a suffering victim, we let go of
living in a world populated by enemies and victimizers, and we let go of an
inner world of hate, recriminations, hopelessness and despair, accusations,
blaming, and disempowerment. Then we can open ourselves up to a world of
love, empowerment and abundance, free to hold open the space for that which
is to reveal itself, in the inner knowledge that that which is can only be good,
positive, loving, and for everyone's benefit.
—Jane Ilene Cohen, Defining the New Paradigm
www.JaneCohen.net

If you aren't good at loving yourself, you will have a difficult time loving anyone,
since you'll resent the time and energy you give another person that you aren't
even giving to yourself.
—Barbara De Angelis

The willingness to accept responsibility for one's own life is the source from which self-respect springs.
—Joan Didion

Believe in yourself and what you feel. Your power will come from that.
—Melissa Etheridge

Always be a 1st rate version of yourself instead of a 2nd rate version of someone else.
—Judy Garland

Health-Esteem is a process of discarding sick-making lessons in our lives and replacing them with healthy thoughts and actions. Critical lessons come from the lives we live. Everything we need to know to initiate healing is available by accessing the data banks of our lives. We are everything that has happened to us.
—Judith Parker Harris, Speaker
Author "Conquer Crisis with Health-Esteem "

Always be a first-rate version of yourself.
—Audrey Hepburn

I don't feel like my money or my success defines me.
I've always been very happy just bein' me.
—Lauryn Hill

A person's worth is contingent upon who he is, not upon what he does, or how much he has. The worth of a person, or a thing, or an idea, is in being, not in doing, not in having.
—Alice Mary Hilton

There is nothing noble about being superior to other men.
The true nobility is in being superior to your previous self.
—Hindu Proverb

I am only one; but still I am one.
I cannot do everything, but still I can do something.
I will not refuse to do the something I can do.
—Helen Keller

Love... when we love and accept ourselves, we shine. To shine, we must be true
to ourselves whether it be in our choice of career, expressing our truth during a
conflict, or taking care of ourselves. Self-love is the foundation of any sparkle
we hope to create in this world. And when we love and accept ourselves, we
create sparkle for all to see.
—Annmarie Lardieri, www.RelationshipRenaissance.com

When one is a stranger to oneself, then one is estranged from others, too.
—Anne Morrow Lindbergh

Before you can get what you want from others,
you have to first be willing to give it to yourself.
—Mary Marcdante, Speaker, Author "Living with Enthusiasm"
www.MaryMarcdante.com

I am convinced that what has the greatest meaning for us
is what we uncover for ourselves.
—Elizabeth O'Connor

Healthy pride is the pride that allows you to feel good about yourself—
pleased, dignified, even bold. It's like confidence, only more centering,
more loving, more personal. Healthy pride provides the sense that you love
yourself just the way you are. You respect and cherish yourself. It's natural.
It's relaxed. It is a gentle presence, that flows from your essence and
allows you to WALK TALL.
—Peggy O'Neill, Speaker, Author "Walking Tall:Overcoming Inner Smallness
No Matter What Size You Are"
Small Miracles Unlimited, www.YoPeggy.com

You teach people who you are by the way you treat yourself.
—Lynn Pierce, Author "Change One Thing, Change Your Life; A Personal
Transformation System" and "Getting to YES Without Selling; The YES System"
www.ChangeOneThing.com

Self-esteem is only one of the factors that should be considered when we look to develop ourselves. Another factor is self-acceptance including loving ourselves, or at least not negatively judging ourselves, when we feel helpless, inferior and vulnerable. Self-esteem alone does not determine your ability to live your life fully. You are a unique human being. You should know what is good about you, accept your strengths and carry them with you into the world. Love who you are becoming.
—Marcia Reynolds, Speaker, Author "Capture the Rapture:
How to Step Out of Your Head and Leap Into Life "
www.OutsmartYourBrain.com

No one can make you feel inferior without your consent.
—Eleanor Roosevelt

Your outer beauty only shows
when your inner-beauty overflows!
—Marilyn Sherman, Speaker, Author "Whose Comfort Zone Are You In?"

Self-esteem isn't everything;
it's just that there's nothing without it.
—Gloria Steinem

I have always regarded myself as the pillar of my life.
—Meryl Streep

To the world you may be one person
but to one person you may be the world.
—Unknown

Think highly of yourself, for the world takes you at your own estimate.
—Unknown

Self-esteem comes from walking through fear.
—Francine Ward, Speaker
Author "Esteemable Acts: 10 Actions for Building Real Self-Esteem"

Service

It is by spending oneself that one becomes rich.
—Sarah Bernhardt

Service is the rent we pay for the privilege of living on this earth.
—Shirley Chisholm

You cannot hope to build a better world without improving the individuals.
To that end, each of us must work for our own improvement and,
at the same time, share a general responsibility for all humanity,
our particular duty being to aid those to whom we think we
can be most useful.
—Madame Marie Curie

Everyone needs to be valued.
Everyone has the potential to give something back.
—Diana, Princess of Wales

. . . you will discover you have two hands;
one for helping yourself,
and the other for helping others.
—Audrey Hepburn

Find a need and fill it.
—Ruth Stafford Peale

A life devoid of service to others is a life devoid of meaning.
--Marianne Williamson, Author "A Woman's Worth"

Smiles

If you have only one smile in you, give it to the people you love.
Don't be surly at home, then go out in the street and start grinning
"Good morning" at total strangers.
—Maya Angelou

Never underestimate the power of your smile to change another person's life.
A smile can put a life back together in an instant.
—Mary Marcdante, Speaker, Author "Living with Enthusiasm:
How the 21-Day Smile Diet Can Change Your Life"
www.MaryMarcdante.com

The most important thing you can put on every morning is your smile.
—Kay Presto, Speaker, Author "Create the Magic in YOUR Life"
Contributor to "Chicken Soup for the NASCAR Soul"

Smile at each other; smile at your wife, smile at your husband,
smile at your children, smile at each other- it doesn't matter who it is-
and that will help you to grow up in greater love for each other.
—Mother Teresa

A smile is a light in the window of the soul indicating that the heart is at home.
—Unknown

A winning smile makes winners of us all.
—Unknown

It takes 26 muscles to smile, and 62 muscles to frown.
—Unknown

Smile; it the second best thing one can do with one's lips.
—Unknown

Soul

If you could only see — What your inner being reveals to me
Your sensitivity is like a fine wine — Your soul is Divine
Thank you for showing me what life is all about
You have shown me that the small things are what count
—Lisa R. Delman, Author "Letters from the Heart"
www.HeartfeltMatters.com

If you lived in The Land of I Can, what would you be doing today?
What does your Soul ache to do? You Can. Anyone Can.
—Susan L. Gilbert, Speaker, Author "The Land of I Can"
www.SusanGilbert.com   www. UnityProducts.com

What is common to all expressions of genuine enthusiasm is that they are
heartfelt and honest, and they uplift our soul and sustain our spirit.
—Mary Marcdante, Speaker, Author "Living with Enthusiasm:
How the 21-Day Smile Diet Can Change Your Life"
www.MaryMarcdante.com

When the light in your soul is on and your heart is full of love,
You radiate an "energy" that is a blessing from above!
—Sue Podany, speaker, author "Energy . . . 120 Easy Ways to Get It, Keep It,
and . . . Keep From Giving It Away!"
www.SuePodany.com

Treasures are always present, often as a vailed essence, waiting to be
acknowledged. Concealed to the stifled heart, jewels of the awakened soul.
—Julie Roy, Co-author of "ABC's of YES! ~ Actions For Success"
www.MagicOfYes.com

Speak from your heart and people will want to be
in the company of your words.
—Sandra Schrift, Professional Coach
www.schrift.com

Sparkle - Tude Boosters

Today, we need little attitude "boosters" to help us overcome negative thoughts and actions that so easily creep into our daily lives. We were born with passion, a natural zest for life, curiosity, playfulness and grace. These "Sparkle-Tudes" help us rejuvenate that unbridled excitement, spirit, and joyful expression:

1) Start off the day on a positive tone.
How we wake up in the morning sets the pace for the rest of our day.

2) Have only positive thoughts toward yourself and others.
Guard carefully your thoughts . . . Attitude, or our truest belief about things, is that highly powered magnet that either attracts – or repels!
Life is composed of our moment-by-moment thoughts.

3) Look for the good in yourself and others.
The Universal principle is that whatever thoughts we have about other people, these are also true of ourselves, as we are all connected, and we are all one.
What we see in others are reflections of ourselves.

4) Believe in yourself, your talents, and your unique gifts.
You were given significant strengths, and have developed skills to support those – use them!

5) Don't to take things "personally."
If something happens during your day, simply observe how you are feeling, and reframe the situation or event in either a positive or neutral manner.
Let it go and move on!

6) Affirm a spirit of gratitude throughout the day.
Start off the day with positive affirmations and anticipations of the day.
I say, "Thank you God, for the gift of this glorious day. I rise, rejoice and am glad in it. Thank you for every way in which I experience your love. I give thanks that my every thought, word and act is only loving and supportive." End the day summarizing all the blessings you received – and watch them multiply!

7) Utilize these unconditional support systems to keep your balance, perspective and sanity: Pets; Faith; Passion Hobbies; and Special People.

— Sheryl Roush, Speaker, Author "Sparkle-Tudes!" and contributing author to "The Princess Principle: Women Helping Women Discover Their Royal Spirit"

The spirit of man is an inward flame;
a lamp the world blows upon but never puts out.
—Margot Asquith

But the fruit of the Spirit is love, joy, peace, patience, kindness, goodness,
faithfulness, gentleness and self-control.
—Galatians 5:22-23

Whether we name divine presence synchronicity, serendipity,
or graced moment matters little. What matters is the reality that
our hearts have been understood. Nothing is as real as a healthy dose
of magic which restores our spirits.
—Nancy Long

Enthusiasm is the language of the spirit.
—Mary Marcdante, Speaker, Author "Living with Enthusiasm:
How the 21-Day Smile Diet Can Change Your Life"
www.MaryMarcdante.com

When we allow our repressed difficult emotions to express and release
in a safe way, without hurting ourselves or others, we reconnect with our
essence, our spirit. We can then regain our wholeness and access our
essential qualities like love, peace and strength.
—Peggy O'Neill, Speaker, Author "Walking Tall:Overcoming Inner Smallness
No Matter What Size You Are"
Small Miracles Unlimited, www.YoPeggy.com

"YES!" is my favorite word.
"YES!" expresses my exuberant spirit. I manifest a life overflowing with love,
peace and joy when I focus on "YES!"

—Julie Roy, Co-author of "ABC's of YES! ~ Actions For Prosperity"
www.MagicOfYes.com

Spiritual Beliefs

It is this belief in a power larger than myself and other than myself
which allows me to venture into the unknown and even the unknowable.
—Maya Angelou, American poet, writer, and actress

I'm aware that people I have loved and have died and are in the spirit world
look after me.
—Diana, Princess of Wales

See God in every person, place, and thing, and all will be well in your world.
—Louise L. Hay

Nothing ever is or was, but is in a state of becoming.
—Mona M. Moon, Speaker
www.MonaMoon.com

Those occurrences called hocus-pocus, 'airy-fairy-woo-woo'
or just plain nonsense by some are simply scientifically explainable events
yet to be discovered.
—Sally Scobey, Speaker, Author "Treasures from the Deep: What I Always
Wanted to Tell My Child"

Write your plans in pencil but give God the eraser.
—Unknown

There will be no peace as long as God remains unseated
at the conference table.
—Unknown

Because God is everywhere, you can pray anywhere.
—Unknown

Stay at Home Moms

You Can Have It All

A Message of Hope for Women
Who Choose to Stay Home with Their Children

1. MAKE THE MOST OF YOUR LIFE EXPERIENCES. No matter what happens in your life, grow from those experiences. Don't allow difficult situations to diminish you or your dreams.

2. CHOOSE A PRIMARY FOCUS FOR EACH STAGE OF YOUR LIFE AND BE INTENSELY COMMITTED TO IT. A primary focus gives you a FRAME for the way you approach the world.

3. NO MATTER WHAT YOUR PRIMARY FOCUS IS, ALWAYS MAKE SURE THAT YOU ARE IN SOME WAY KEEPING YOUR PROFESSIONAL SKILLS ALIVE. Read current writings in your field, rent tapes from the library, talk to others periodically who are still working full-time in your area of expertise, attend conferences and workshops, go back to school part time if you possibly can.

4. RE-EVALUATE YOUR PRIORITIES AT LEAST ONCE A YEAR, ALWAYS KEEPING THE LONG TERM IN MIND. When the time is right to change priorities and focus, communicate that clearly to others and make decisions that support that change.

5. BE CREATIVE. Whatever your life situation may be, do the very best you can within the focus you've chosen.

6. NETWORK CONSTANTLY. Get to know people in your community, your church, schools. Let your skills and talents be known by others. Then, when your focus changes, you will already have a group of people who can recommend you.

7. BELIEVE IN YOURSELF AND YOUR DREAMS. Even though you may have chosen to put your career "on the back burner" for a while, always approach each life task or experience like a professional.

—Barbara A. Glanz, Speaker, Consultant, Work/Life Balance Expert
Author "CARE Packages for the Home—Dozens of Ways to Regenerate Spirit Where You Live" and "Balancing Acts: More Than 250 Guilt-free, Creative Ideas to Blend your Work and your Life"
www.BarbaraGlanz.com

Stress

When stressed or going through a difficult time, it is essential that you take the time to relax in order to replenish your mind, body, and spirit. Nurture your well being by creating an oasis of calm in your life. Getting calm allows you to get a fresh perspective and helps you cope better physically and emotionally with your troubles. Being able to control at least one aspect of your life, in this case time to yourself, helps you to get a grip on the rest of it. For success, take the "t" out of "can't."
—Anonymous

ALL STRESSED OUT AND NO ONE TO CHOKE
—Bumper Sticker

Yes, I've heard of "decaf."
What's your point?
—Bumper Sticker

Everything seems worse when you're tired.
—From the book "Cancer for Two" for Caregivers
www.CancerForTwo.com

Take the **STING** out of feeling overwhelmed:

Select one task you've been putting off.
Time yourself. Give the task one full hour.
Ignore everything else. Focus on doing just this one task.
No breaks allowed.
Give yourself a reward when the job is done.

—Rita Emmett - Recovering Procrastinator
Author "The Procrastinator's Handbook and The Procrastinating Child: A Handbook for Adults to Help Children Stop Putting Things Off"
www.RitaEmmett.com

When we think of emotions as traffic "yield" signs telling us to
slow down and pay attention to what we're feeling, they work for us
instead of controlling us.
—Mary Marcdante, Speaker, Author "Living with Enthusiasm:
How the 21-Day Smile Diet Can Change Your Life"
www.MaryMarcdante.com

I've discovered there are two kinds of people in the world:
people with conflict, and dead people.
And I've learned that if you don't learn how to deal with it in the first group,
you quickly end up in the second.
—Catherine Tucek

Do your best and let God do the rest!
—Unknown
(Submitted by Elisa Castaneda)

Stress is the enemy. It reduces your capacity for engaging your fun self.
— Leslie Yerkes, Co-author "301 Ways to Have Fun at Work"
Author "Fun Works: Creating Places Where People Love to Work"

Success

Formula for Success:
Write down your goals, share them with others and visualize your success before it happens.
—Debbie Allen, Speaker , Author "Confessions of Shameless Self Promoters"
www.DebbieAllen.com

Success is liking yourself, liking what you do, and liking how you do it.
—Maya Angelou

Success is a state of mind.
If you want success, start thinking of yourself as a success.
—Dr. Joyce Brothers

For you to be successful, sacrifices must be made.
It's better that they are made by others but failing that,
you'll have to make them yourself.
—Rita Mae Brown

BEHIND EVERY SUCCESSFUL WOMAN IS HERSELF
— Bumper Sticker

Success today is not just a matter of what we accomplish but the overall process and positive experience.
—Donna Fisher, Speaker, Author "People Power"
www.DonnaFisher.com and www.OnlineBusinessNetworking.com

Success is normally inconvenient. (Working long hours.)
—Sandra Golden

Enthusiasm, however you define it, is at the core of all success.
Whether you're hoping to achieve a big dream, heal your body,
find peace of mind, influence a client to choose your product,
push for a promotion, derive more pleasure from your community or church,
or have deeper committed relationships with those you love,
enthusiasm can help.
—Mary Marcdante, Speaker, Author "Living with Enthusiasm:
www.MaryMarcdante.com

The only thing standing between you and what you want in life, is you.
You can achieve what you want in life if you're willing to put your mind,
heart and energy into it.
—Debra Pestrak, Speaker, Author "Playing with the Big Boys"

If your success is not on your own terms, if it looks good to the world
but does not feel good in your heart, it is not success at all.
—Anna Quindlen

Your potential, whether it be intelligence, ability, or whatever, is only a small
part of the equation of success; it's what you do with your potential that makes
the difference.
—Teresa Norris

God doesn't require us to succeed; He only requires that you try.
—Mother Teresa

Success comes before work only in the dictionary.
—Unknown

Success is not a doorway, it's a staircase.
—Dottie Walters

I am grateful for the blessings of wealth, it hasn't changed who I am.
My feet are still on the ground. I'm just wearing better shoes.
—Oprah Winfrey

Taking Risks

If you play it safe in life, you've decided that you don't want to grow anymore.
—Shirley Hufstedler

And the trouble is, if you don't risk anything, you risk even more.
—Erica Jong

Life is either a daring adventure or nothing.
—Helen Keller

It is better to be boldly decisive and risk being wrong
than to agonize at length and be right too late.
—Marilyn Moats Kennedy

"How does one become a butterfly?" she asked pensively.
"You must want to fly so much that you are willing to give up
being a caterpillar."
—Trina Paulus

There is strength in our feminine softness.
We do not need to be anything that which we are not.
When a woman OWNS her own power - no man can stand up to it.
Be your unique and authentic self: "Step INTO your Greatness.!
— Sheryl Roush, Speaker, Author "Sparkle-Tudes!" and contributing author to
"The Princess Principle: Women Helping Women Discover Their Royal Spirit"

If you are never scared, embarrassed, or hurt,
it means you never take chances.
—Julia Soul

Don't be afraid to go out on a limb.
That's where the fruit is.
—Unknown

If your life is free of failures,
you're not taking enough risks.
—Unknown

If you want to stand out, don't be different,
be outstanding.
—Meredith West

Buyers are graded not only on their successes, but also on their failures.
Too many hits means the buyer isn't taking enough chances.
—Leslie Wexner

What you risk reveals what you value.
—Jeanette Winterson

Nothing great in history was ever accomplished without risk.
The risk for great success is the same as the risk for failure — extremely high;
the risk involved in producing mediocrity is extremely low.
To succeed greatly, we must risk greatly.
Risk is inherent in innovation and innovation is the life-blood of our future.
Lead the way into the future — don't follow.
— Leslie Yerkes, Contributor to "Business: The Ultimate Resource"
Co-author "Beans: Four Principles for Running a Business
in Good Times or Bad"

Talents

I believe that talent is like electricity.
We don't understand electricity. We use it.
You can plug into it and light up a lamp, keep a heart pump going,
light a cathedral, or you can electrocute a person with it.
Electricity will do all that.
—Maya Angelou

I've never sought success in order to get fame and money;
it's the talent and the passion that count in success.
—Ingrid Bergman, Swedish actress

I have filled you with the Spirit of God, with skill, ability and knowledge
in all kinds of crafts.
—Exodus 31:3
Women's Devotional Bible 2, New International Version

If you have a talent, use it in every which way possible.
Don't hoard it. Don't dole it out like a miser.
Spend it lavishly, like a millionaire intent on going broke.
—Brenda Francis

We find our calling or it finds us, and it's a sin against the fates
not to use your talent when you have it.
—Erica Jong

Work on bringing out a special trait that you admire about yourself
and don't let anyone stop you from being like that.
— Michelle C. Roush, age 16
From an essay entitled "To Be Free"

Teaching

Teachers open the door, but you must enter by yourself.
—Chinese Proverb

I believe that children are our future.
Teach them well and let them lead the way.
Show them all the beauty they possess inside.
—Whitney Houston

Teach to the problems, not to the text.
—E. Kim Nebeuts

Teach others as they need to be taught.
Meet people where they are, and communicate on that level.
Speak to the heart, not the head.
—Sheryl Roush, Speaker
www.SparklePresentations.com

A master can tell you what he expects of you.
A teacher, though, awakens your own expectation.
—Unknown

Time

Take time to think
It is the source of power.
Take time to play
It is the secret of perpetual youth.
Take time to read
It is the fountain of wisdom.
Take time to laugh
It is the music of the soul.
Take time to work
It is the price of success.
Take time to give
It is too short a day to be selfish.
Take time to pray
It is the greatest power on earth.
—Anonymous

For everything there is a season,
And a time for every matter under heaven:
A time to be born, and a time to die;
A time to plant, and a time to pluck up what is planted;
A time to kill, and a time to heal;
A time to break down, and a time to build up;
A time to weep, and a time to laugh;
A time to mourn, and a time to dance;
A time to throw away stones, and a time to gather stones together;
A time to embrace, and a time to refrain from embracing;
A time to seek, and a time to lose;
A time to keep, and a time to throw away;
A time to tear, and a time to sew;
A time to keep silence, and a time to speak;
A time to love, and a time to hate,
A time for war, and a time for peace.
—Ecclesiastes 3: 1-8

You cannot manage time, you can only manage tasks.
—Linda Brakeall, Author "Unlocking The Secrets of Successful Women in Business" and "The Respected Woman Series"

It is important from time to time to slow down,
go away by yourself, and simply be.
—Eileen Caddy

Time is a fixed income and, as with any income, the real problem facing most of us is how to live successfully within our daily allotment.
—Margaret B. Johnstone

1,440 minutes in a day.
Take some for you.
—Cath Kachur, Speaker, Artist
www.HumanTuneUp.com

There is no such thing as time management.
Time just is. Instead, learn to manage your life.
It's actually easier to accomplish.
—Maria Marsala
www.ElevatingYou.com

Time is God's way of keeping everything from happening at once.
—Unknown

There's no time like the present to do what you want to do.
—Oprah Winfrey

Trust

I had to admit that my "perfect" childhood left me with hurts, disappointments and blocks that needed to be healed.
I had to admit that this individual who pretended to have it all together was really a frightened little girl who wanted someone to tell her that she was lovable even if she wasn't perfect. I came to learn that this message needed to come from me.
—Colette Carlson, Speaker, Contributing author, "Conversations on Success"
www.colettecarlson.com

Begin to weave and God will give you the thread.
—German Proverb

If you want more of something—
you need to give it first.
If you want more recognition—
you need to recognize others first.
If you want others to trust you—
you need to trust them first.
If you want others to love you—
you need to love them first.
—Sheryl Roush, Speaker, Author
www.SparklePresentations.com

Trust your gut.
-Barbara Walters

Truth

You never find yourself until you face the truth.
—Pearl Bailey

We don't have to trample other people's feelings to express our own –
speak your truth, speak from your heart for caring connections.
—Colette Carlson, Speaker
Contributing author, "Conversations on Success"
www.colettecarlson.com

Favorite word: "Truth."
—Barbra Streisand, interviewed on Screen Actor's Guild

You cannot change the truth, but the truth can change you.
—Unknown

I believe in the sun even though it is slow in rising.
I believe in you without realizing.
I believe in rain though there are no clouds in the sky.
I believe in truth even though people lie.
I believe in peace though sometimes I am violent.
I believe in God even though He is silent.
—Unknown

Say it unto others as you would have them say it unto you —
and for heaven sakes, don't take too long to get to the point.
—Joni Wilson, Voice Expert, Author "The 3-Dimensional Business Voice"
www.JoniWilsonVoice.com

If you do not tell the truth about yourself,
you can't tell it about other people.
—Virginia Woolf

Unconditional Support

4 Simple Ways to Nurture Yourself and Keep Your Sanity

Women have numerous gifts to give to the world today — especially in times like these. Yet, if we are not nurtured ourselves, life becomes more challenging, difficult and unbalanced. In order to enlighten, nurture and heal others — we must first do these things for ourselves.

Here are four simple ways to help keep balance in our daily lives, so we are able to be there for others. According to stress management experts, we have four support systems available that offer us unconditional love and support.

1) Pets
Pets are nonjudgmental, forgiving, sensitive and supportive. They instinctively KNOW when we need a hug or are feeling emotional, depressed and upset, and don't run at the first sign of tears! Medical research even proves that hugging a pet lowers blood pressure, and helps to rebuild the immune system.

2) Faith – Spiritual Belief System
This inner compass enables us bring forth that wisdom, authenticity and insight into all we do on a daily basis. These beliefs ground and center our moral foundation, offering direction, and trust to walk to our path in this world.

3) Passion Hobbies
Passion Hobbies are pastimes that nurture our spirit and balance our lives. Reading; walking, dancing, running, aerobics or exercise; crafts; puzzles; playing with kids; or shopping!

4) Special People
These may be relatives, or significant others, still be living, or have already made their transition. Highly supportive kindred spirits. We can pick up conversations with them, right where we left off, without missing a beat.

You have numerous gifts to give to the world today — and those gifts are needed in times like these. Nurture yourself first, and those challenges become easier to handle, with less stress and more love. Utilize these simple unconditional support systems to bring you more balance and joy in your daily life.

—Sheryl Roush, Speaker, Contributing Author to "The Princess Principle"

United We Stand

If

(In memory of September 11th, 2001)

If everyone is glued to the news
Worried about what is happening far over seas,
If everyone is trying to find a few clues
As to find why someone far away would now be pleased,

If the people around you are angry or upset
At the events that have taken place,
And wanting to help others that they have never met
Which prior in our country was an unusual case.

If our elected leader vows retribution
For the awful deeds that were done,
If he is determined to find the means in our constitution
Promising that those responsible will never again have fun,

If the rest of the world shows us compassion
Backing our nation all the way,
Each lending help in their own fashion
Uniting the world with the event of one awful day.

If those found guilty are hunted down
And prosecuted for their crimes,
Will there still be on everyone's face a frown
A lingering reminder of these horrid times?

If it takes a tragedy so great
To unite people everywhere,
Then let us all stand together before it's too late
And show the world that Americans do care!

—Serina Roush, age 17—

Values

Don't expect your children to do
anything you won't do for yourself.
—Colette Carlson, Speaker
Contributing author, "Conversations on Success"
www.colettecarlson.com

Christmas is not a date.
It's a state of mind.
—Mary Ellen Chase, American writer (1887-1973)

I am, at last, marching to my own drum, connected to what I love most.
And, I am 100% committed to the directions I am now taking.
Frankly, that is all that matters.
—Jovita Jenkins, Author, Coach, Speaker
www.JovitaJenkins.com

As we discover and dialogue about what we value
(what is important to us),
we free ourselves to create the experiences that match them.
Without that knowledge, life is one unconscious choice after another
that may or may not get us what we truly want.
Talk about what's important to you and keep choosing,
moment by moment, to do what is important to you and you will,
step by step, find your success.
—Mary Marcdante, Author "My Mother, My Friend: The Ten Most Important
Things to Talk About With Your Mother"
www.MaryMarcdante.com

The beauty in knowing your values is that whenever you're in doubt
about a decision you need to make, you simply ask yourself:
"Does this choice support my core values?"
If the answer is yes, it's a clear choice to make
(although not necessarily easy to implement,
which is why sharing your values with your support system is so helpful).
If your choices do not support your values,
then it's a matter of reprioritizing what is most important
or making new choices.
—Mary Marcdante, Author "Living with Enthusiasm:
How the 21-Day Smile Diet Can Change Your Life"
www.MaryMarcdante.com

You demonstrate your values and beliefs daily
by the way you live your life.
—Lynn Pierce, Author "Change One Thing, Change Your Life"
www.ChangeOneThing.com

What is important is simple:
Know what you value and invest your time accordingly.
This is integrity and it will bring you peace.
—Rhoberta Shaler, PhD
www.OptimizeLifeNow.com

We can tell our values by looking at our checkbook stubs.
—Gloria Steinem

The least of things with a meaning is worth more in life
than the greatest of things without it.
—Unknown

Vision

No vision and you perish; No Ideal, and you're lost;
Your heart must ever cherish some faith at any cost.
Some hope, some dream to cling to,
Some rainbow in the sky, Some melody to sing to,
Some service that is high.
—Harriet Du Autermont

Create a vision of the life you want to create -
make it so clear and so vivid that when you close your eyes
you see it on the inside of your eyelids.
That vision will pull you forward and the steps you must take
to make it your reality will magically appear.
—Rebecca Everett, Speaker, Author, Coach

Build it and they will come!
—From the Movie, Fields of Dreams

Vision without action is a daydream.
Action without vision is a nightmare.
—Japanese Proverb

Let your vision encompass the grandest ideals, the most spectacular notions,
and the highest truths. Let your dreams be bigger than life. Because anything is
possible!
—Peggy O'Neill, Speaker, Author "Walking Tall: Overcoming Inner Smallness
No Matter What Size You Are"
Small Miracles Unlimited, www.YoPeggy.com

Reach high, for stars lie hidden in your soul.
Dream deep, for every dream precedes the goal.
—Pamela Vaull Starr

Perception creates reality.
The outside world mirrors whatever is in inside you.
—Barbra Streisand, interviewed on Screen Actor's Guild

Do not follow where the path may lead.
Go, instead, where there is no path and leave a trail.
— Unknown

Three levels of organizational vision:
1. The Do-able
2. The Conceivable
3. The Previously Unthinkable
— Unknown

Visualization

Don't just sit back and wait for things to happen to you –
make things happen with visualization and a strong focus
on your goals and aspirations.
—Debbie Allen, Speaker
Author "Confessions of Shameless Self Promoters"
www.DebbieAllen.com

Ordinary people believe only in the possible.
Extraordinary people visualize not what is possible or probable,
but rather what is impossible.
And by visualizing the impossible,
they begin to see it as possible.
—Cherie Carter-Scott, Speaker

I train myself mentally with visualization.
The morning of a tournament, before I put my feet on the floor,
I visualize myself making perfect runs with emphasis on technique,
all the way through to what my personal best is in practice . . . .
The more you work with this type of visualization,
especially when you do it on a day-to-day basis,
you'll actually begin to feel your muscles contracting
at the appropriate times.
—Camille Duvall

TOP TEN THINGS ONLY WOMEN UNDERSTAND:

10. Cat's facial expressions.

9. The need for the same style of shoes in different colors.

8. Why bean sprouts aren't just weeds.

7. "Fat" clothes.

6. Taking a car trip without trying to beat your best time.

5. The difference between beige, ecru, cream, off-white, and eggshell.

4. Cutting your bangs to make them grow.

3. Eyelash curlers.

2. The inaccuracy of every bathroom scale ever made.

AND,
the Number One thing only women understand:

1. OTHER WOMEN

One is not born a woman, one becomes one.
—Simone de Beauvoir

We must not, in trying to think about how we can make a big difference, ignore the small daily difference we can make which, over time, add up to big differences that we often cannot foresee.
—Marian Wright Edelman

Toughness doesn't have to come in a pinstripe suit.
—Dianne Feinstein, on women's role in government
quoted in *Time* magazine, June 4, 1984

Parents can only give good advice or put them [children] on the right paths,
but the final forming of a person's character lies in their own hands.
—Anne Frank, "The Diary of a Young Girl" (1952) entry for July 15, 1944

The problem that has no name - which is simply the fact that American women
are kept from growing to their full human capacities - is taking a far greater toll
on the physical and mental health of our country than any known disease.
—Betty Friedan, Author "The Feminine Mystique"

I now know all the people worth knowing in America, and I find no intellect
comparable to my own.
—Margaret Fuller

Oprah interviewed Dolly Parton and asked if the size of her breasts
were ever an issue...."These?!? I call these my massive distraction."
—Dolly Parton

I am Woman, hear me roar!
—Helen Reddy

Born a precious child, our Life beckons to find the wise woman inside,
only to show us the truth about our lives is to remain that precious child,
after all.
—Sheryl Roush, Speaker, Author "Sparkle-Tudes"
www.SparklePresentations.com

Worrying

Do not worry about what others say
Throw it all away
Follow your truth
You will see
Your inner gifts shine through
In everything you do.
—Lisa R. Delman, Speaker, Author "Letters from the Heart"
www.HeartfeltMatters.com

Stop worrying about the potholes in the road
and enjoy the journey.
—Babs Hoffman

Prepare for what you want to happen,
not for what you are afraid might happen.
—Barbara C. Lemaire, PhD
www.NextStepCoaching.com

May the sun bring you new energies by day,
may the moon softly restore you by night,
may the rain wash away any worries you may have.

May gentle breezes refresh your soul and all the days of your life,
may you walk gently through the world and know its beauty.
—Unknown

Worry is the misuse of imagination.
—Unknown

When you spend your life worrying about how other people feel,
you lose track of how you feel.
—Unknown

Worry is like a rocking chair,
it will give you something to do,
but it won't get you anywhere.
—Unknown

Blessed is the person who is too busy to worry in the daytime,
and too sleepy to worry at night.
—Unknown

Definition of worry: "duress rehearsal."
—Unknown

Zen

If you understand, things are just as they are;
if you do not understand, things are just as they are.
—Zen Proverb

The obstacle is the path.
—Zen Proverb

The world is like a mirror, you see?
Smile, and your friends smile back.
—Zen Proverb

The Master in the art of living makes little distinction
between his work and his play, his labor and his leisure,
his mind and his body, his education and his recreation,
his love and his religion.

He hardly knows which is which.
He simply pursues his vision of excellence in whatever he does,
leaving others to decide whether he is working or playing.

To him he is always doing both.
—Zen Buddhist Text

Sheryl Roush

Sparkle-Tude™ Expert Sheryl Roush presents inspirational programs that rekindle the spirit, raise the bar, and create excitement.

Humorous, creative and authentic, she relates real-life experiences in a positive, lighthearted way that enriches the soul. She playfully engages audiences, offering valuable how-to tips while entertaining with stories, songs and surprises. Audiences don't "hear" Sheryl speak -- they "experience" her presentations - with lasting feelings and significance.

She was only the third woman in the world to earn the elite status of Accredited Speaker as honored by Toastmasters International (now in seventy countries) for outstanding platform professionalism. Sheryl was crowned "Ms. Heart of San Diego" for 2004-2005.

Audiences consistently jump to their feet with standing ovations from Sheryl's inspiring, heartfelt, life-changing messages. Participants throughout Australia, Canada, England, Malaysia, Northern Ireland, Puerto Rico, Singapore, and the US have awarded her top-ratings for content, impact and delivery style.

She has presented at Conferences including:
Baptist Healthcare
Catholic Congress
California Lutheran University - Creative Options-A Day for Women
Central California Women's Conference
Clemson University's Professional Women's Conferences
Institute of Real Estate Management
Los Angeles Unified School District's SuperStars
San Diego Charger Cheerleaders
Sharp Hospital Women's Health Symposium
Women in Business Expo
Women in Publishing Society-Hong Kong

Bring her to speak at your conference - as a keynote and breakout session, customized workshops, special events and facilitating retreats.

Sparkle Presentations
Sheryl@SparklePresentations.com
www. SparklePresentations.com
Call Toll Free (800) 932-0973 to schedule!

*Are low morale, high-stress and poor attitudes
affecting your customer service, productivity and teamwork today?*

Need to rekindle the spirit on your organization?

Bring in Ms. Sparkle-Tude™ to energize positive trends!

Programs include:

Sparkle-Tude!™ Keeping a Sparkling Attitude Every Day
·Discover 7 Sparkle-Tude™ Boosters for home, work and life
·Learn how to deal with difficult people and challenging situations
·Enjoy 67 ways to stay sane and lighthearted in stressful times

Creating a Positive Work Environment
Tips and ideas to bring positive attitudes, connection and spirit to work

Customer Service with Heart
Enhanced communication skills and attitude-boosters to generate authentic
and exceptional service.

Humor in the Workplace
Discover tips to build morale, teamwork and cooperation, boost creativity, and
lower mistakes while bringing lightheartedness into your organization.

Audiences include:

AT&T
Cal State-Northridge
ChildStart
Ernst & Young
IBM
Intuit/Turbo Tax
Kiddie Academy
McMillin Realty
Mitsubishi
7-Up
SCORE and SBA
Sheraton
SONY
Union Bank
Verizon Wireless
Westin Hotels
YMCA
and *Y--O--U!!!*

Sparkle-Tudes!

Index

Sparkle-Tudes!

Order Form

[ ] Audio "Attitude is Everything!"
   Keeping a Smile on Your Face When the Day Gets You Down!.. $15.00
[ ] Audio "Assertive Communication Skills for Women" $15.00
[ ] Audio "Perc-U-Lating Power: Having More Passion & Purpose"............................. $15.00
[ ] Audio "Solid Gold Marketing Tactics"....(for target marketing, direct mail) $15.00
[ ] Audio "Sparkle-Tude: Women in Business" (live program)..................................... $15.00
[ ] Audio "Sparkle When You Speak" (customized for women) Public speaking skills............. $15.00
[ ] Book "Solid Gold Newsletters" how-to design brochures, fliers, handouts $20.00
[ ] Book "Sparkle-Tudes!" Inspirational Quotes By and For Women $14.95
[ ] Book: "The Princess Principle: Women Helping Women" $20.00
   18 stories of courage, hope, faith.......... Chapter entitled "Sparkle-Tude " by Sheryl Roush
[ ] CD "Attitude: The Healthy Alternative" (customized for women)................................. $15.00
[ ] CD "Solid Gold Marketing Tactics"....(for target marketing, direct mail) $15.00
[ ] CD "Sparkle-Tude: Women in Business" (live program)...................................... $15.00
[ ] Video "Attitude: The Healthy Alternative" (customized for women) $29.95

SUBTOTAL: $_____
California residents 7.75% sales tax: $_____
Shipping & Handling: $_____
ORDER TOTAL:$_____
Please add shipping of: $5.00/first item; $3.00 each additional item

Name _____
Mailing Address _____
City_____
State/Province_____ Country _____Zip _____+_____
Telephone (_____) _____
e-mail : _____

[ ] Author Autograph-- personalized inscription to read:
_____

Make checks payable to: Sparkle Presentations
Credit cards welcome: [ ] MasterCard   [ ] Visa   Expiration date _____ / _____

Card # _____

Sparkle Presentations
P.O. Box 2373, La Mesa, CA 91943 USA
Sheryl@SparklePresentations.com
www. SparklePresentations.com
Phone orders: (858) 569-6555
Fax orders: (858) 569-5924

Spirit Voyage's

KUNDALINI TRANSFORMATION KIT

YOGA AND MANTRAS FOR PROSPERITY

BRING WEALTH AND ABUNDANCE INTO YOUR LIFE

by GURUGANESHA SINGH AND KARAN KHALSA

ISBN-10: 0983569517
ISBN-13: 9780983569510

About the Kundalini Transformation Kit

SPIRIT VOYAGE has created the Kundalini Transformation Kit series to offer a set of meditations and principles to live by to support your life's needs. This tool kit incorporates Kundalini Yoga as taught by Yogi Bhajan®, whose powerful yogic technology supports so many aspects of our day-to-day lives.

It is our hope that using these tool kits will provide you with a source to improve your life and transform it into the manifestation of your hopes for your self and your soul.

Spirit Voyage believes that music has the power to transform the planet, one person at a time. By incorporating the beauty of the sound current into these yogic meditations, we use the technology of Naad yoga to create a vibration that imprints the impact of these meditations deep into the psyche.

You can use these meditations one by one, practicing each one for 11 to 40 days, or you can use them in combinations, practicing them at different times of day. Create a sacred space in your home to practice these meditations. Allow yourself to immerse yourself in the experience of them.

WE WISH YOU DEEP AND POSITIVE TRANSFORMATION!

CD TRACKS

Music for Prosperity

1. BOUNTIFUL, BLISSFUL, BEAUTIFUL
by GuruGanesha Singh and Snatam Kaur ~
Prosperity Affirmation

2. PROSPERITY HAR by Prabhu Nam Kaur & Snatam Kaur ~
Powerful Prosperity Meditation

3. BAHOTA KARAM by Sat Hari Singh and Hari Bhajan ~
Nanak's Abundant Gifts Meditation

4. ARDAS BHAEE by Mirabai Ceiba ~
Meditation for Your Life's Needs

5. HAR HAR HAR HAR GOBINDAY by GuruGanesha Singh ~
Fearless Prosperity Meditation

TABLE OF CONTENTS

The Guiding Principles of Prosperity by GuruGanesha Singh

The Guiding Principles of Prosperity Consciousness

By GuruGanesha Singh

To me, prosperity is a flow. I live my life doing things that keep me in the flow and avoiding things that block the flow. Playing music puts me in the flow, and I devote my life to that. Prosperity is a flow, not just from the Universe to you, but also from you to the Universe. Giving puts you into the flow and creates the opening for you to receive. For me, music is both. I receive so much from the Universe when I play music, and I know that I give back to the Universe through playing music. This is what we all need to find for ourselves, and prosperity will abound.

Prosperity consciousness is very much a state of mind. You must have trust in the flow. You must trust that if you give, you will receive. Then you can spend your life focusing on doing what fulfills you, knowing you will in turn be completely taken care of.

For a spiritual person, I recommend the entire focus be the prayer "Thy will be done. Dear Lord, how can I best serve?" Not on money. For the last 40 years, I have continuously prayed to my guardian angel and teacher, Guru Ram Das. Whatever has come before me, I put my full energy into excelling at it, even when it came to washing dishes in my first ashram in 1973. After two to three months of negativity, when I embraced the mantra and the teachings, I felt an overwhelming sense of gratitude.

I believe that in my life, I have been prosperous because I have zero fear that I'm not going to be provided for. It doesn't matter what your net worth is. If you believe everything is going to be provided for, you are a prosperous person. If you are in a state of fear that there's not going to be enough, that fear is the opposite of prosperity consciousness. Prosperity comes from faith and conviction that you and the universe are one. Look at the birds; they are not worried. They just fly. They know the wind will lift them up and carry them to their destination. That is what my life has been like for a long time. We must trust that the Divine will lift us up and carry us to our destination.

Many paths revere poverty as a path to the Divine. My teacher, Yogi Bhajan, always taught that prosperity opens the doorways to many things. If you revere poverty, you will probably remain impoverished. I've never been reluctant to make a lot of money. I've followed the guiding principles of prosperity throughout my life, and as a result, I've been able to use the abundance I have received to in turn give back in many ways. You have to have the conviction that if a lot of money comes to you, it would be in the best interest of the Universe. If you don't believe that, then you will sabotage anything that could bring you a lot of prosperity. You must know, at your core, that if prosperity comes to you, you will use it to serve.

Many people believe that money corrupts, and it can. But you don't need to believe it will corrupt you. The real art is generating success, and not being corrupt, having incredible integrity and becoming a great giver. You must continue to live by the guiding principles of prosperity, even when you achieve financial wealth, or you will soon lose it.

I don't think you need to have money to be happy. I think that happiness comes from being fully engaged in the flow of the Universe. When you are so engaged in the here and now, so fully present and focused on your daily work of doing and giving and receiving, that you are not worrying about the past or desiring things from the future, then prosperity can flow your way. That's why every sacred path tells you to sing God's praises. When you are singing with all 72 trillion cells, you are fully in the present and fully in the flow. The Universe can't help but take care of you.

Over the course of my life, I have learned through trial and error what opens me up to the flow of prosperity. In these pages, I have focused those things into ten unique principles to live by. These are the guiding principles of prosperity consciousness that I live by. Try them. You will see that abundance starts to flow your way.

GUIDING PRINCIPLE 1:

Have a Daily Practice to Strengthen the Self

I believe you need to nourish your soul on a daily basis. I believe that the soul is the core of all of one's being; it's the best part, the yolk in an egg, the highest self, the essence. The soul is where the most goodness is, the most light, the most kindness, the most compassion, and the more we bathe in that part of ourselves, the more we radiate the qualities that produce the most positive and magnificent life possible. You need to feel good about yourself to have a positive relationship with your soul.

One of the main reasons that you have a daily practice is to slowly build up your self-image. If your sense of self is low, it doesn't matter what you engage in, a high percentage of your thoughts will be accompanied by self-limiting beliefs. As you raise your self-image, it will be much easier for you to keep up and deal with adversity as it manifests.

When you get up in the morning, you need to start with a victory, whether it's taking a cold shower and then doing a strenuous yoga practice, or lacing up your sneakers and going for a run, or going to the gym and working out or taking a swim. You need to start the day with a victory. It builds momentum. Start with little victories and before you know it, big victories will manifest.

That's why the best time to do your daily practice is first thing in the morning, upon waking up, because it gives you this victorious feeling that carries over.

GUIDING PRINCIPLE 2:

Do Something that is True to Your Core

Do something that you have no duality about. Do something that every one of your 72 trillion cells believes is good for the entirety of existence. Then, it has to be good for you. Do something that you truly believe is in the best interest of your divine self and of the whole planet.

I've been doing sales training for years, and I can speak from my core to my students in a sales training class, but I can also pick up a guitar and be true to my core, or I can talk to my son and be true to my core as a parent. You bring your unique self to all your different roles in life. If you can feel that you are being true to your core in all aspects of your life, then you will find prosperity in every one of them.

There is a difference between being in love with a job and recognizing that you are doing something that is true to your core, something that is in harmony with your inner integrity. Whatever it is you are doing you need to be excelling at. I've always been a subscriber to the "s#*t or get off the pot" mentality. Don't hang around in a state of duality. You do not serve yourself or the people around you.

If you do not have conviction in what you are doing, then you've got to find something else, take the risk, and make the switch.

GUIDING PRINCIPLE 3:

Have Enough Conviction in the Self to Take Risks

You must believe in yourself, in your ability to recognize what is true to your core, and in the fact that what you choose to do is going to serve yourself and the Universe. Then, you must follow your true inner voice and understand what you are being called to do, and take that risk to do it!

When you know that you are doing something that is true to your core, there is no risk, because your choices are based on what is most important.

When you take a risk, you must be ready to handle the worst-case scenario. When I say "take a risk," you must ask yourself what is the worst thing that can happen? You might fail ... but then you take another risk and start something else. And eventually, if you are being true to your core, you are going to succeed.

Your actions are a manifestation of your beliefs. If you have conviction in yourself and you have conviction in your ability to succeed and be victorious, you will find a way to overcome every adversity.

GUIDING PRINCIPLE 4:

All Your Communications Must Radiate Good Will and Integrity

100% of your communications! 99% is not good enough, because if 1% of your communications are negative, it can wreak havoc on your universe. You can spend so much of your valuable time cleaning up the mess that the 1% created.

One ill-executed communication can take up so much of your valuable time. Have you ever said something to someone that maybe didn't come from the most positive space inside you, and then spent hours and hours and days and days cleaning up the mess?

Maintaining good will always serves you because your reputation precedes you. Additionally, if you do everything from a place of integrity, deep down you feel really, really good about yourself. Start fresh today living in integrity. I don't need to explain that. The word integrity just resonates.

There's an old expression that the hard way is the easy way and the easy way is the hard way. The easy way is to just get something done as long as you're feeling okay about it. But if you have not ensured good will all around, that ends up being much more difficult. It's worth taking on the extra work of ensuring everyone feels good.

Remember, good will and integrity must be constant and prosperity will follow.

What are you waiting for? At the end of that road is bliss.